THE SELF-PUBLISHING BLUEPRINT

A COMPLETE GUIDE TO HELP YOU SELF-PUBLISH YOUR BOOK

DANIEL WILLCOCKS

PRESS

OTHER TITLES BY DANIEL WILLCOCKS

Non-fiction for Authors

Collaboration for Authors

The Self-publishing Blueprint

Fiction

They Rot (The Rot: Book 1)

They Remain (The Rot: Book 2)

When Winter Comes

Twisted: A Collection of Dark Tales

The Mark of the Damned

Sins of Smoke

Anthologies

The Other Side

The Omens Call

Keep up-to-date at

www.danielwillcocks.com

For every individual with a story in your heart.
The only limit is your own belief.

FOREWORD

SACHA BLACK

Apparently, Dan and I met twice at various 20Booksto50k conferences before I actually acknowledged his existence—I'm not sure whether that says more about me or him, but it is what it is. It wasn't until a mutual friend flung us into an awkward messenger group and promptly introduced us that we started talking.

We'd both left our day jobs at the same time—okay fine, technically he left 10 days before me, which he periodically likes to prod my competitive side with. But the point was, we were both at a similar place in our businesses with freelance work and book publishing, so we made a good match.

Roll on a few months of writing sprints and publishing chats and one of us (I suppose I'll give Dan the credit) said "I've got an idea." We have since learned that phrase is to be handled with caution. It must be whispered and caressed like a lover because it's dangerous—it has power like nitrous oxide and rocket fuel. Ten minutes later the Next Level Authors podcast was born—a podcast neither of us had time for but were both diving head first into.

And I'm so glad we did.

A year later and Dan is one of my best friends; he's taught me so much about mindset and what I'm really capable of. So, when he asked me to write this foreword, I couldn't resist the chance to encourage you to read on. Yes, our friendship is full of banter, but underneath there is an enormous foundation of respect. I count myself extremely lucky to have Dan in my life. He's a daily inspiration to me, whether that's through his monstrous productivity, how he constantly strives to help more authors, to improve his coaching, or to give more back to the community.

If you've picked up this book then you're in for a treat. Dan imparts a mountain of wisdom he's gained over the last six years of publishing. He takes you step by step through finishing the book, editing, formatting, designing covers, uploading, and actually publishing the darn thing. He shows you mistakes to avoid as well as best practices to follow, and all with a liberal sprinkling of humor.

This is the ultimate guide to get you from completed book to hold-in-your-hands published novel. It's funny and uplifting but at the same time lays out every step you need to take to fulfill your publishing dream.

I don't say this lightly, but if a writing career is what you want then you don't just want this blueprint, you need it.

Sacha Black, The Rebel Author
www.sachablack.co.uk
April, 2021

1

LIGHTS, CAMERA, PUBLISH
OR "WHY CHOOSE SELF-PUBLISHING?"

 A book is a dream you hold in your hand.

— NEIL GAIMAN

S o, you want to self-publish a book, eh?

You've got an idea tickling the back of your squishy gray matter and you want to see that idea materialized on paper? Well, much more than paper. You don't want to just write a twelve-page essay and print it out on a scrap of A4 from your Canon printer, do you? You don't have plans to hand your mother, or friend, or son, or colleague a one-inch-thick stack of papers with the ramblings of your fictional masterpiece for them to scribble over or to use as shredded hamster bedding, or fuel for their campfire?

No.

You want to publish a goddamn *book*.

I'm excited for you.

Do you know why?

Because this dream of yours is more than possible for *anyone* who wishes to hold their creation in their hands. Poets, essayists, novelists, teachers, chefs, crochet artists (because it *is* an art, don't argue), memoir writers, veterans, engineers, and virtually anyone who has something to say can publish a book these days—and that is a beautiful thing.

Self-publishing has revolutionized the way that the publishing industry works. In the years of yore (or, approximately fourteen years ago, if you want to be specific), *waaaa*y back in 2007, the Amazon Kindle was first released. This little electronic device that was kind of like a handheld tablet, but also wasn't, because it had this weird e-ink stuff that kind of worked like that toy you had as a kid that was basically a plastic board filled with blunt needles, and when you pressed your hand into its surface it left an impression of your hand in the blunt metal ends, though most of the time people actually pressed their faces into, well, I did anyway, sometimes my tongue, too...

Where was I?

Oh, yeah. Kindles.

The Amazon Kindle shattered the centuries-old tradition of how publishing was expected to work. Pre-2007, in order to get your book published, you really only had two options:

- You could go directly to a publisher or an agent and have them vouch for your work, buy into your idea, wait several years for that idea to become a reality, and then, after all that wait, and *hope* that you reached author superstardom (which was much rarer than people think. I've spoken to a *lot* of mid-list authors who were published by big publishing houses who never quite struck the success of Dan Brown or Suzanne Collins).

Or...

- You could become a vanity press. You could purchase a thousand copies of your book, stock the boxes at a dangerous height and angle in your garage or shed or spare bedroom or loft, and then try to sell those copies yourself—hardly the most efficient way to flog your book...

If this all sounds like a lot of effort, that's because it is. In truth, traditional publishing is still very much a gate-keeper-centric force to be reckoned with. If you like the idea of having Penguin Random House or HarperCollins back your seedling of a story idea, then you're still very much going to be fighting an uphill battle. It's 100% still possible to continue down that route, but there is now another option available to you.

Hell, I hope you already know this. It may just be why you've picked up this book.

What Is Self-publishing?

Self-publishing (often referred to as "independent" or "indie" publishing) is simply the act of taking your publishing journey into your own hands. Self-publishing is your way, as a creative, to stick your middle finger up to the gate keepers and the nay-sayers of this world in order to have your work published and attempt to reach the audiences that you wish to reach.

Self-Publishing Is Cheating, Though. Right?

Self-publishing has earned a bad rep over the years, particularly in the earlier days of Amazon's pioneering "Kindle Direct Publishing" service.

In the beginning, before the algorithms became more sophisticated and people worked out the kinks of this brand-new superpower, the online book charts were littered with badly written books, poorly edited manuscripts, questionable book covers, and a whole range of books with other issues. The author community raised concerns around maintaining the *quality* of the books that people wanted to read. To be able to tell the difference between a self-published book in 2010, and a traditionally published book was like being able to tell the difference between a yo-yo and a tomahawk. There was no comparison. One you could "walk the dog with," the other you could murder a dog with.

Please don't confuse the two.

Over time, as with all great things that skyrocket to success, the market began to mature. Self-published authors began to realize the mistakes they were making, and to imitate the books that the big publishing houses had been putting out for years. In the wake of immense demand, editors and cover designs and proofreaders sprang up out of their little hobbit holes and started to actually help the self-publishers. It became impossible for readers to tell the difference between a book that had been through a publishing house with a staff base of over 200 individuals, and a forty-something mom of five who was publishing her book from her bedroom/office in the tiny slithers of time granted to her in her manic day of toddler wrangling, school runs, and part-time job.

At the same time as this, Amazon began to work out the

kinks of their magical algorithms. Reader reviews and popularity of books were taken into account to ensure that they were only advertising the books that people actually wanted to read. Their storefront charts went from being a display window at a crumbling OXFAM to mirroring the reckoning forces of Barnes & Noble and Waterstones.

Now, some fourteen years after the initial launch of the Kindle, the publishing landscape has taken a cataclysmic shift. Self-published books are taking the markets by storm and giving the big publishers a run for their money. Throughout the coronavirus pandemic, in a time in which bookstores were closed and unable to sell physical copies of novels, big publishers actually studied self-published authors, turning to the tactics that these formerly laughed-at authors have been employing for nearly a decade. Digital sales are through the roof on eBooks, there are more tools available than ever to help you self-publish a *professional-*looking book, and there are so many platforms in which you can advertise your work to your readers, that it's almost unimaginable.

What was once a humble little "try-hard" cult, has since blossomed into its own booming industry. If you've seen names in the book charts like Hugh Howey, Joanna Penn, Shayne Silvers, Michael Anderle, Dakota Krout, L.J. Ross, Adam Croft, Adam Nevill, E.L. James, Andy Weir, and Amanda Hocking (to name a few), then you may not even realize that you're staring at *self-published* authors who have all made a living from writing and are well-respected in their craft. Self-published authors who have sold millions of books, some with film adaptations from their works, most making well over six figures a year, even a few who have been picked up by traditional publishing houses and now have deals which help boost their work.

We live in an amazing time in history in which the digital world can help us achieve incredible things. No longer are we funneled through a media lens and told what is and isn't possible. All you have to do is jump online and do a little bit of your own research to find out what the limits of the publishing industry truly are.

Can you find your own audience in 2021?

Yes.

Can you self-publish a book that will help you quit that day job?

Yes.

Can you have real-world impact with the stories and the tales that you wish to tell?

Yes.

Absolutely.

Without question.

I don't know how else to say this to you without sounding like a cheesy 4am commercial.

Writing and publishing a book isn't easy but, thanks to the advancements of that last decade, *you* can make it happen.

Yes, you.

Don't look over your shoulder, I'm talking to *you*.

All it takes to self-publish your book is a dollop of elbow-grease, a sprinkle of know-how, and the dogged determination to put your best foot forward and make it happen.

Wait—How the Hell Do *You* Know All of This Stuff?

I self-published my first book in 2015, a little-known stage play that I had written during my university years. That book did nothing in the way of sales or making a name for who I am, but it accomplished one very important goal for me: it proved that I could publish a book by myself and list it on the Amazon store.

My next venture was a little bigger than that first play. In October of 2015 I self-published my first horror novella, *Sins of Smoke*. I had formerly spent two years as a proofreader and copy-editor for other people's creative works, and I wanted to try my luck at getting my own story down on paper.

Little did I know back then that that book would go on to hit the #1 spot on the Amazon horror charts throughout the Halloween period, and springboard a publishing career that saw me leave my day job in 2019, co-write with some of the biggest names in independent fiction, start a multi-million downloaded fiction podcast, become a book coach, and write over forty pieces of fiction across a number of novellas, anthologies, and novels.

I owe everything I have to self-publishing and the opportunities that it brings. I've seen the successes, and I know the possibilities that lie in those tiny pixels embedded on your computer screen.

Who knows, if I do my job right with this book, maybe soon you will, too.

A Glimpse at What's to Come

The pages before you are loaded with a host of useful information to help you make your introduction into the self-publishing arena. Over the last few years, I've worked with dozens of authors to help them get started on their self-publishing journey and, although each author was writing in a different genre, with an overall different goal of what they wanted to achieve from their books, one major concern kept propping up along the way:

 "How do I know what I don't know?"

It's a valid concern, and one that can paralyze budding authors, either through fear or intimidation of the unknown. It's all well and good saying that you plan to *write* a book, but how do you do the rest of it? What if you forget a major step along the way and you publish a book riddled with spelling and grammar errors? What if you screw up your formatting and you have blank pages that get slammed in reviews? How do you approach finding a team of advanced readers to help you launch your book? What if I overpay for a service that delivers crap results?

The entire concept for this book sprang from that one, single concern. A simple *knowledge gap*, if you will. In the upcoming chapters, I will provide a step-by-step guide to all of the basic steps of how to self-publish. I will take you from the conception of your book (because self-publishing starts before you write a single goddamn word) to what happens after you've clicked "Publish." This book will serve as an initial blueprint to see your idea turned into a reality that you can hold in your bare hands.

You don't have to do this alone. I've got your back.

Six Million Dollars and a Dump-Truck Full of Elephants

I can't promise to give you that. No one can.

This book will not teach you how to get rich quick and live your dream of hand-raising elephant calves.

This book will also not teach you how to *write* a book.

The subject of writing craft is comprehensive, varied, and thoroughly covered throughout a number of works available on any bookstore. Yet, the subject of how to *self-publish* that finished book is one that isn't given a lot of attention.

It's all well and good knowing you have to write the book, but what about the rest of it? *That's* what I'm going to cover. If you want to learn the mechanics of craft, story, theme, plot, structure, and all that good stuff, I've certainly got some resources in the pages ahead that will help, but I'll defer you to the masters on that one.

Stop Rubbing the Lamp, I'm Not a Genie

While I do lay out every step that stands before your path of getting your book published and displayed on the digital bookshelves, this is not a "get rich quick," or "90 days to fame" book. Though there are strategies and methods to make good money with your self-publishing, this book will focus on the practicable steps to actually getting your work out into the digisphere.

Along the way, I will lay bare all of the "Pro tips" and tricks that I have learned along the way to set you up for success—after all, why half-ass your self-publishing journey when you can create a professional, quality book that at least stands a chance at making it? These tips will help you position your book in the best possible way to make money and get seen in today's publishing market...

...but the rest is down to you.

How hard are *you* willing to work? What do *you* want to achieve with your book?

Hold on... I may be getting ahead of myself, here. Let me finish this chapter with a simple, cliché, John Hammondstyle entry as the gates open up and the John Williams' symphony strikes their crescendo.

Clears throat.

Welcome, my friend, to ~~Jurassic Park~~ my Self-Publishing Blueprint.

SUCCESSFUL WRITERS STUDY

OR "MARKET RESEARCH FOR YOUR BOOK"

> *A moment's insight is sometimes worth a life's experience.*
>
> — OLIVER WENDELL HOLMES JR.

Why? Why, Mum! Why?
Or "Understanding Your Why"

You're right to question your motivations. After all, there's an unspoken motivator and reason behind everything that we do. It's a beautiful sunny Friday morning in the UK as I write this, and I *could* be outside walking. I *could* be continuing my battle to learn how to juggle four balls (I'm fairly confident with three, but I want to expand, so sue me). I *could* be watching *Parks & Recreation* on Netflix, or phoning my sister to see how she's getting on post-op from her gall bladder removal.

But I'm not doing any of those things.

Why?

Because I'm a horrible person?

I'm not. I promise. I called her yesterday. She's fine.

It's because I want to write this book.

"Why?" you may ask.

"Because I want to help authors," I may reply. "Because I want to shrink the knowledge gap that comes with the daunting task of self-publishing a book—and self-publishing that book *well*." I've personally gained more than I could ask for through my own experience of self-publishing, and I want to give back to a community that has given me a chance to live a free, independent life making a living with my words.

Your "Why" may be different.

There are a number of common reasons I see for why people choose to write their books. Chiefly, those are:

- **Dollar, dollar bills, y'all:** Many authors see the dollar signs when they think of publishing their book. They look at the names listed at the top of the charts, the authors who have had their works turned into movies and plays and adapted into other media, and they want a slice of that cake. They dream of trading their day job for whiskeys on the porch and mornings at the typewriter, exchanging their words for cold, hard cash.

- **Documentarianism:** Some authors have lived a Life—yes, with a capital "L"—even at a young age. They have a unique story to tell. They want to share the unusual with the world and open up about real-world experiences that can be shared and placed into the public eye—whether that's just to their grandkids, or to stadiums of eager fans.

- **Look at me now, Dad!:** Who hasn't dreamed of being publicly revered for their work? Whether it's an award, a certificate, a medal, or reaching the top of a bestsellers list, public acceptance and the approval of respected peers can be the ultimate goal for many authors.
- **Keep it secret, keep it safe:** Maybe the examples above make you shudder and retreat into the corner. Maybe you're like me and how I began my journey, wanting nothing more than to simply hold your humble book in your own hands and sniff the pages (we all do that, right?). You don't need achievement or coin, or for anyone else to even see your book. All you want to know is that *you've written a book* and it fits perfectly into that space you've reserved on the shelf for the last forty years. After all, who wouldn't want to write something that'll outlive them and tell their story for years to come?

Whatever your reason to publish, it would benefit you greatly to know, to at least some degree, what kind of outcome you wish to have with your book. If you think about your end result *before* you pen a single word of your narrative, you're giving yourself the best chance at creating a book that achieves what you'd like to achieve.

For example: if I wanted to make "Dollar, dollar bills, y'all," I would need to pay close attention to which books are currently selling in the charts and *why* they are. I would need to look in-depth into the types of book covers that resonate with the ideal reader. I would need to thoroughly understand the genre tropes, reader social platforms, promotional sites, and any methods and tactics associated with those particular kinds of books by writers who are killing it in that area.

(While this book won't go in-depth on that kind of write-to-market approach, bestselling author Chris Fox's *Write to Market: Deliver a Book that Sells* is a great resource which covers all of the basic principles.)

Whereas, if you wish purely to have your book sit on your bookshelf for you and you alone, a lot of these principles won't apply. You can write and do whatever you want. You'll still find plenty of useful information ahead, you'll just need to frame the information to suit your particular Why.

"You've Got to Hooold on to What You've Got..."
Or "Making it Through the Hard Parts"

Knowing what you want your outcome to be from your book will help you hold onto your idea when the going gets tough.

Writing a book isn't easy. There's a reason why 97% of writers never finish their book. There's a reason why 99% of those who *do* finish their book will never publish it.

Writing is elating, but it's also a slog. It's beautiful, but it's also soul-crushing. It's joyous, and it's frustrating. When times are good, the words fly from your fingertips as though you've been possessed by the spirit of Jim Carey in *Bruce Almighty*. When the times get tough, all you want to do is hurl your Commodore-64 out of the window and, with any luck, crush your neighbour's pesky cat that keeps you up until 3am with its yowling.

Two birds, one stone, and all that...

Your Why is your life raft. It's the thing that will keep you afloat when all you want to do is curl up on the sofa and thumb through your telebox. If you know your Why... Like, *really* know and understand and embody and absorb your Why, you'll be able to reach the end of your book, and you'll have a chance at achieving your goal.

Want my advice? (Of course you do, that's why you're reading this book.) *Write down* what you're doing all of this for. Put it on a sticky note and place it on your computer screen. Tattoo it on your forehead. Brainwash your children to parrot back your Why as their morning mantra when they first open their eyes.

Whatever it takes to get your engine going and make this happen... Do that.

Wouldn't You Rather Be Watching Netflix?
Or "Why This Book? Why Now?"

Similarly to understanding your own personal Why, you need to think about the Why of your book.

Why this book? Why now? Why, out of all the possible scenarios and ideas, do you want to put *this* book into the world?

Is it because you're deeply passionate about the fictional story you wish to tell?

Is it because you've seen the rising rate of knife crimes in East London and you believe that this book will speak to those hard-to-reach groups and have a real influence on reducing the crime rate?

Is it because your nana is one of the last surviving women of work from World War II and you want to capture her legacy for your descendants to read in years to come?

Whatever your reason, now is the time to think about what this book is going to bring you and the world. Take some time to sketch out a few reasons as to why you're choosing to write this book, right here, right now.

After all, time is precious. You want to make sure you're using it wisely.

Yes, That's All Very Lovely, Daniel. But Who's it For?
Or "Your Ideal Reader"

When writing your book, you need to know who's going to be on the other side of the page, sitting by the lamplight with a steaming mug of Joe beside them.

You can't write a book that will please everyone. If you try, you'll please no one.

That's a fact.

Every audience has their own way that they like to be spoken to. If you're explaining quantum physics to an eight-year-old, you're probably not going to go into detail about the hydrophobic charge of anti-ions and their relationship with the nucleic acids associated with sodium-fluoride...

(Yes. I failed my Chemistry A-levels. I'm sorry.)

No. You're going to find a way to speak to little Tammy so that she understands what you're talking about. You create analogies with dodgeballs or cookie dough or Minecraft blocks to give her the basic principles of what you're trying to say.

Alternatively, you don't want to speak to Albert Einstein in a cutesy, baby voice, explaining how he's been a good boy for not dripping that yellow stuff on the rim of his big boy potty.

Now, *there's* an image.

My point is that your audience will dictate the type of book you wish to write. If you want your book to have the maximum amount of impact and success, then you need to speak to the people you're trying to reach. You can go really niche with your non-fiction, and aim your book at 36- to 43-year-olds who have been dreaming of cycling in the Alps, or you can be more vague with your fiction and just say that you're trying to hit horror fans (although, even horror has its buckets of sub-genres. Are you writing an occult story, or one of psychological suspense? Each reader wants their own thing).

No matter who you're aiming your book at, make sure that you're aiming at *someone*. I know that when I'm writing my horror books, I'm writing horror for *me*. I'm my own audience, because I know the sub-genres of horror that I like, and I know that I'm not the only one in the world who enjoys the stuff that I do. Friends of mine write in fantasy, and appeal to those who are always hungry for the likes of *Game of Thrones* and *The Lord of the Rings*, huge expansive worlds filled with threat and politics and a good sprinkle of dragons.

Once you know who you're aiming your book at, you've set your North Star. Carving a path to a specific destination is infinitely easier than blindly strolling along the side of the M25 motorway and hoping that you end up in Brixton. Once you know your end goal (combining your *Why* with your *Who*) then you've already done more than many writers who choose to introduce a book into the world have done. You've increased your chances of success ten-fold.

I'm proud of you, kiddo.

Move Aside, Pratchett. You're in My Way
Or "The Winning Publishing Mindset"

For the record, I have nothing against Terry Pratchett. That guy was (and remains) an icon, and one hell of a gifted writer (may he Rest In Peace).

If you're looking to make some kind of real impact with your books, you're going to have to topple the towers of the greats. You're going to have to find the giant so that you can stand on her shoulders and reach the people who you want to reach.

You're not an island. The world of writing is filled with thousands of author-minnows attempting the exact same thing that you're trying to do. Every one of them is swimming around and trying to get to the surface, trying to chomp on the yummy food that rains down from above them.

But in order to break through the ranks, you have to outsmart the bigger fish.

In order to outsmart the bigger fish, you have to first *identify* them. You have to *understand* them. You have to learn their ways, discover what it is that they're doing that you can emulate. You need to know them inside and out in order to gain your creative edge and surpass them.

Okay, I'll jump out of the fish metaphor for a moment.

The book chart algorithms favor the intelligent players among them. When writing your book, you need to understand the genre inside and out. If you're looking at writing a book that sells, you need to know what is currently trending and selling, and you need to know who the big-named authors are in your arena that you'll need to rise above in order to out-sell them. When I first started writing my books, I browsed the charts for a few weeks to work out the names that stuck around. I noted the authors who were consistently selling good books (most importantly, books that *I* wanted to read), and I watched them.

Like a hawk.

Looking down over a jetty.

Teeming with minnows.

Oh, yeah. Look at that clever circle-back to the analogy...

There's no point watching Jo Bloggs if his books aren't selling. There's no point studying Theresa Shelby if she's writing in a completely different genre to you.

You need to understand *your* market; your genre, your competition, your mini corner of the book world. Once again, this kind of attention to detail early on in your book writing career will pay back dividends and help inform the kinds of books that you are going to write. Sure, maybe your motivation *isn't* to write a book that tops the charts and brings in Scrooge McDuck levels of coin, but if you want to write a book that people enjoy—like *really* enjoy—then it's well worth studying those who are slaying the craft. If I ever want to learn to bake, I'm going to find a baker who understands the nuances of proofing dough and oven temperature when baking the perfect... ciabatta? (Okay, so people don't read these books for my perfect examples, but you get the general idea.) I'm not going to go to my next door neighbor's niece who once watched the *Great British Bake Off* and thinks she's mastered the craft just because she's grasped the basic principles of a bain-marie.

It's not just about "hacking" your way to success. It's about informing your road ahead. The more knowledge you can glean of what does and doesn't make a good book in the genre and fields you're trying to reach, the greater your chance of success.

Battles are won in the war room, not on the battlefield.

Great books begin *before* a pen touches the page.

Set the foundations. Gather the knowledge. Know what it is that you're letting yourself in for. Only then can you truly begin to write the book you're hoping to write.

PRO TIP: If you're keen to explore a few genres to find where you want to plant your flag, services like Publisher Rocket are a great way to see how particular genres, keywords, and categories are performing in the charts.

Look! A Penny!
Or "Setting Your Budget"

One last piece of advice before you set forth on your journey of authorship: set your budget.

You're about to take your first steps into a world of self-publishing. That means that you are creating a *product* that you will be putting out into the world. People can buy your product, exchange it for currency, hold the tangible leaves of paper in their hands.

With the creation of your product, there will inevitably be costs.

"How much does publishing a book cost?" you might ask.

The answer is a simple one, as much or as little as you are willing to invest in making the book as professional as you can.

Is it possible to create, edit, and publish a book for free?

Absolutely.

Is it advised?

In my opinion, no.

Throughout this book, I will highlight some of the main costs that are associated with book publishing. Chiefly among these, you'll want to allocate funds toward editing and book cover design. When it comes to marketing your book post-publishing, there are ways to do this for free, though putting money on the table will certainly heighten your chances of success.

We'll get into this in more detail later in the book. For now, scribble down a rough figure of what you believe you can afford. Bear that number in mind as we move ahead.

The advantage of writing a book in today's publishing climate is that there are low-budget options and premium-budget options for all areas of self-publishing. As I mentioned in the previous chapter, there is *no* barrier to self-publishing. If you're broke and you want to publish your memoirs. You can make that happen.

For *free*.

If you're filthy rich and want to invest in the best and the greatest of everything in order to compete with the James Pattersons and the Harper Lees of this world, then go ahead.

This is *your* journey.

These are all steps to help *you* have the greatest chance of success with your book.

Why wouldn't you want to make the best damn book you're capable of making?

3

ALL THE NUTS AND BOLTS

OR "PLANNING YOUR BOOK"

   First, find out what your hero wants, then just follow him!

— RAY BRADBURY

A s I mentioned in Chapter 1, there are thousands of books out there that can teach you the mechanics of how to write a book. There are courses, there are conferences, there are blogs and online essays. From novel writing to non-fiction, one can perform a quick Google search to find thousands of ways to improve your craft.

I'm not going to go deeply into all of the intricacies of writing the book. That's better left to the masters, and I promised to show you how to *publish* the book, not how to *write* it. If you want a few recommendations of books that have vastly helped with my own writing, then here are just a few that I often recommend to writers (in no particular order):

- Blake Snyder's *Save the Cat*
- Sacha Black's *Anatomy of Prose*
- Libbie Hawker's *Take off your Pants*
- Joanna Penn's *How to Write Non-fiction*
- Stephen King's *On Writing*
- J. Thorn and Zach Bohannon's *Three Story Method*
- Dean Wesley Smith's *Writing into the Dark*
- Becca Puglisi & Angela Ackerman's *The Emotion Thesaurus*
- Chuck Palahniuk's *Consider This*

That said, for those who would like a few notes on the cornerstones of what comprises a good story, I'm happy to sow some seeds in order to pique your curiosity. Sometimes it helps just to know where to *begin* your educational journey on craft.

After all, what follows are all critical components of a well-structured book.

Twiddling Your Mustache in Your Underpants
or "Plotting vs Pantsing"

Rule number one of writing: there is no "write" or wrong way to tackle your book (see what I did there?).

Writing is a solo venture, and therefore you must capitalize on what it is that fuels *you*. You need to understand how *you* work, and how *you* perform at *your* peak levels.

And therein comes the "pantsing versus plotting" debate.

To "pants" a book simply means to write without too much of a roadmap before you. Also referred to as "discovery writing," the pantsers of this world thrive off the unknown. Pantsers will often start a book with a vague sense of where they are going to go (sometimes with no idea at all) and will simply write the story as it comes to them. Their characters lead the way, the world unfolds itself, and their story is born from a magical mix of stardust, luck, and good circumstance.

Stephen King, Chuck Wendig, and Margaret Atwood are classic examples of pantsers.

Margaret Atwood generally starts with "...an image, scene, or voice... I couldn't write the other way round with structures first. It would be too much like paint-by-numbers."

David Morrell, "like[s] to think of the book as being an adventure. I have this mantra which says, Serve the story, listen to the story. And often the story knows better than I do what it wants to be."

This is all well and good for those who can place their fingers on the keyboard and race off into the sunset. But what about those who thrive off outlines and structure ahead of the creation of the book?

Well, these people we call "plotters." Sounds sinister, doesn't it? Or maybe that's just my default position as a natural pantser...

Plotters *need* to know the journey ahead before they take it. Plotters are the family members who print off sheets of itinerary pages ahead of a vacation. They know the agenda for each day, they know where all the local town resources are before they've landed, they know how to get here, there, and everywhere weeks ahead of the journey—because it's important to them.

It's the same with their books. Plotters will generally have a comprehensive idea of each character within their book, where the journey is going to take them, and the conflicts they face along the way. They will know the characters as if they were their own friends. They will know the world as if they could walk it with their eyes closed. They *know* the story, long before they've typed the first words of the first chapter.

That doesn't mean that things can't change along the way, but having an outline, knowing the structure, and knowing where each heartbeat of the story *should* be helps a plotter to keep moving forward.

Imagine it this way: pantsers will gladly drive into the dark with only their headlights to guide them, reacting to each new idea and obstacle along the way with excitement and gusto. Plotters will have placed their torches and beacons along the road and will know the full breadth of the journey before they start. Nothing will surprise them, because it's all how it's meant to be—in most cases.

Famous plotters include Joyce Carol Oates, Ernest Hemingway, and Roy Peter Clark.

Joyce Carol Oates says, "The first sentence can't be written until the final sentence is written."

Hemingway argues that, "Prose is architecture."

Whatever your method for writing, it's important to understand that you *can* be either a pantser or a plotter, but that's not where you have to plant your flag. Many writers evolve and change over time, and it's a process of finding what works for you. Chuck Wendig claims to be a reformed plotter after spending years as a pantser in his works. "... some writers are natural pantsers, others are pantsers-by-default, pantsers-by-laziness. They do not plan, they do not outline. They don't because it's hard. And frustrating. And irritating. That's why I didn't used to do it."

Me, personally, I like to think of writing as a spectrum. If a pure pantser sits at number one on that spectrum, and plotting sits at a hard ten, then I'm a three. I have a concept, I know my protagonist, and I have a general theme, but then I just set loose and let the characters do the discovery for me.

I find it much more fun that way.

Have a think about where you sit on the spectrum. You may not yet have an answer. You may find your answer changes over time.

In the Land of Mordor Where the Shadows Lie
or "Choosing Your Setting"

The setting of your world is a character in itself.

Imagine if *The Lord of the Rings* was set in 19th-century England. Imagine if *Gone Girl* was set in the fictional land of Narnia.

Where your book is set matters. The world you create sets the tone for what your readers can expect from your story. If you have an idea for a suspenseful thriller in which you find out that the babysitter was the one "who-dun-it," your book is going to be vastly different if it's set in the frozen Alaskan north compared to the warm tropics of the Bahamas. It's going to turn the book on its head if it's set in a tin shack in the Mid-West as opposed to a twelve-bedroom mansion in Bangkok.

Your setting needs to be appropriate to the story you're choosing to tell. A well-chosen setting can create a flavor and a theme that complements every element of your story. Think carefully about where you imagine your characters to be situated in the world. Be specific about what that setting can bring to your story and how it can heighten the conflicts you introduce. Consider more than just the physical location. Look at the time period. Look at the socio-economic surroundings. Look at the physical space your characters live in.

Throw them all in a pot and get stirring that book in your cauldron.

The Ghosts of Christmas POV
or "Tense and Points of View"

Past, present, future. First, second, third. Omniscient, limited. How are you going to *tell* your story?

I struggled with this one a lot when I first started writing. I would write a chapter in a third person point of view (POV), past tense, then go back and re-write in first-person because I thought it would be better.

It wasn't.

So, I'd change it again.

Then I'd go back.

I would go to present tense, then back to past.

Then back to present.

Then back to past.

The point of view and the tense of your story can have a huge impact on the type of story that you're trying to tell. For those who need some reference points of the options to you, here are the main four points-of-voice you can explore in your story.

- **First person:** You are telling the story as "I." The reader is put directly into the head of the person telling the story and seeing through that person's eyes.

- **Second person:** You place the story upon the reader. The protagonist is "You." While this is the least commonly used in fiction, it can have its advantages depending on the type of story you're telling.
- **Third person (limited):** The characters in the story are other people. They are "he," "she," and "they." With a limited third-person narrative, you still remain close to the character, and are telling the story from their perspective. The reader is only aware of what the character knows.
- **Third person (omniscient):** Here you are writing "he," "she," and "they" characters again but, this time, you have a whole view of the world you are creating. You can write about other characters and their thoughts and feelings, even though your protagonist will be blind to them. This is sometimes known as the "playing God" POV.

The main tenses you can use in your story are:

- **Past:** You are telling a story as if it has already happened. For example, Jim gazed up at the night sky.
- **Present:** You are telling a story that is happening in the here and now. For example, Jim gazes up at the night sky.
- **Future:** You are telling a story that is yet to happen. For example, Jim will gaze up at the night sky.

Knowing the appropriate tense and POV of your story is

fundamental in ensuring that you strike the tone that you are looking to strike with your book.

Many genres tend to expect particular tenses and POVs. For example, thriller books will often employ first person, present narratives to give the reader the impression that the action is happening to the character in the here and now. This immediacy in the narrative amps the tension and pace and keeps the reader lost in the scene. Whereas epic fantasy tends to utilize the third-person, omniscient view with a past tense lens—this allows the writer to explore the full stretch of history of the world and to get lost in all of the wider world-building details that fantasy readers are known to love.

Whatever POV and tense you choose to use in your book, be deliberate about where you start, and make sure it matches the expectations of the audience you are trying to reach.

Just Give Them What They Want
or "Genre Tropes"

Put simply, your readers know what they want to read.

So, give it to them.

"Genre tropes" is a fancy way of saying "reader expectations." They're the heartbeats of the stories that you're used to reading. They're the pulses of familiarity readers have come to expect, but usually don't know that they expect them. It's the universal truth that bonds all stories of a particular genre together.

Your readers love space opera? Give them plenty o' spaceships.

Your readers love post-apocalyptic? Give them desolate

worlds and gritty specificity on survival methods and hazards.

Your readers love romance? Give them some love.

Genre tropes are the key to telling a good story in your chosen niche. You may think that you've got a witty bent on how to make the story unique and different. But readers don't want different.

They want the *same*, but *different.*

For example, if you are writing a thriller, your readers don't want a word-for-word re-telling of *The Girl on the Train*.

They also don't want a thriller that's set on Mars during the French Revolution which tackles the climate crisis and explores the story of a wanna-be chef, featuring elements of splatter-gore.

There's a middle ground to be had here. Readers want the same train journey, but with slightly different scenery. They want the familiarity of the stories they love, with alternate details that blur the edges of their comfort zone. Stephen King and Clive Barker write very similar types of stories, but they write them in their own way. Fans of horror can enjoy both authors, knowing that they'll enjoy the meal while leaving with a slightly different taste in their mouths.

Have a think about the books you love most that are in the same genre and you'll see what I mean. Using horror as an example (in case you haven't gathered what my favorite genre is), horror readers *expect* characters to die in their books—typically in big numbers and in nasty ways. They expect misery and destruction and for the ending to be bittersweet.

Horror readers don't want the monsters to win. But we also don't want the protagonist to have a good time of it, either. If you're writing about a protagonist who effortlessly trumps the monster and then skips off into the sunset, then you've set yourself up for failure, and your reviews will reflect this.

There are tonnes of resources online to help you understand the tropes of your genre. For the plotters out there, these can act as a basic framework to help inform your story. For pantsers, get familiar with them and incorporate them into your process. If you miss any of these tropes on your first draft, work them back into your story in the edits.

You may think that your unique idea is earth-shattering and what the world has been asking to see for years, but if it doesn't match what readers are used to, then you're setting yourself up for failure.

All Aboard!
or "Casting Your Characters"

What would your favorite story be without a smorgasbord of personalities to connect with?

The characters you create are arguably one of the most important elements of your story. They're the conduits through which your reader understands the tale you're trying to tell. They're the vessels which carry the narrative and create the human connection between your fiction and the reader's reality.

Humans connect to humans. We connect to emotion. We connect to the threads that bond us together. (If you're a non-human reading this, replace "emotion" with your species' chosen unifying quality). Without a diverse, interesting, and emotionally resonating cast of vagabonds, the story won't stand on its own two feet.

Be specific about your chosen protagonist. Be deliberate about your antagonist. Be complementary with your side characters. Make sure that your chosen cast delivers the story to your reader in the most effective (and real) way possible.

The Wind Beneath Your Wings
or "Theme and Tone"

Theme is the underlying message that your story tells. It's the bonding glue that holds everything together and gives your story its particular lens.

Common themes in fiction can include: good versus evil, love, redemption, coming of age, to name just a few. They're the overarching rays of morality you throw into your book. If you're telling a story of "love," each scene, each chapter, each beat of your story should speak of love and the struggles and elations associated with it. If you're writing a "coming-of-age" story, you should hinge your narrative on the moments of revelation and irreversibility that come with growing up through a lived experience.

It's advised that you hang your story on one primary theme. In order to have the most impact with your words, you don't want to confuse the reader with too many messages at once. If your chosen theme is "redemption," then go hard on that particular knot in the muscle and work it until it's smooth.

That doesn't mean you can't include dashes of the other themes. If you're writing a "good versus evil" story, you can still have a sub-plot that includes romance for your character, but the overarching theme should always revert back to your original selection.

Tone relates more to a global emotion or feeling.

In horror, your global emotion is likely to be one of

suspense and threat. In romance, it'll likely be optimism and joy. Your tone can be humorous, sad, informal, harmonious, serious, and any other emotion on the feelings wheel.

Think of theme and tone as a way to provide particular colors and flavors to your story. They're the wind beneath the wings that keeps the story afloat as you write it. The stories that have the most impact master these two mechanisms in a way that really delivers the message of your words.

The Backbone's Connected to the Hip Bones
or "Structuring Your Story"

How are you going to tell your story? I mean, the shape of how you tell it.

Do you know how many "acts" you are going to have? Have you thought about your beginning, middle, and end? How are you going to balance all of the pieces in between?

There are countless ways to structure your story. Popular examples of storytelling structure include the three-act structure, the four-act structure, and the five-act structure. Have you discovered Freytag's Pyramid, the Fichtean Curve, or the Save the Cat structure? You could explore the Hero's Journey, or even the *Seven* Point Structure.

I know, I know. How many forms of structure can there truly be?

The important thing to remember about any of these structures is that they are there to help give you more direction with your story. As a consumer of story (whether through reading or watching or playing), you will subconsciously know that the tension, conflict, and stakes of a story rise the further through the tale you get. You don't begin *The*

Lord of the Rings with Frodo standing on the brink of the fires of Mount Doom, about to throw the ring in the fire. That would make for a terrible rest of the film.

No. You make him *earn* it. You slowly raise the stakes as you go through the story, each obstacle growing in size and difficulty, until you have your protagonist in a position where they have to jump through the final ring of fire, over the Canon of a Thousand Needles, diving through the Tunnel of Infinite Poison Dart Frogs, swimming under the Canyon of Catalonian Crocodiles, until, at last... finally... after all of that fuss... they make it.

Because your protagonist *should* make it.

Unless there's a hella good reason not to.

There *are* exceptions to every rule.

Whichever story structure you choose to explore and frame your work within, they all carry the same basic principles and universal truths. The differences are negligible, but they do resonate better with some writers than others.

Explore some of these methods for yourself and choose which one you think will work for you. Remember, you can always try the others on your next project.

But let's not get too ahead of ourselves. First, we've got to write the damned thing.

4

___

THE LYNCHPIN OF YOUR BUSINESS

OR "WRITING THE GODDAMN BOOK"

 The scariest moment is always just before you start.

— STEPHEN KING

This is it.

The main event.

It's what you've waited for.

"Get your butt in the chair and write." Advice I've heard again and again in my career. It's the one thing that we, as writers, know that we must do, yet it's one of the most frustratingly difficult things to actualize.

Putting pen to paper, or fingers to keyboard, or words to dictation device is the lynchpin of any writing career. Words are the building blocks of it all. Without words, the rest of the process is moot. Without an actual effort to get the book down on paper, you're pissing into the wind.

It's self-destructive and stinky.

At this point along your self-publishing journey, there is

little advice that I can give. I can't tell you *what* story to write. I can't tell you *how* to write it.

But what I *can* give you is advice on how to make that first draft shine, and how to actually get the damn book finished.

It's kind of my specialty.

Leave Nothing on the Table
Or "Writing Your Best Book"

Nothing sells a book better than an amazing story.

If there's one thing that I advise you *have* to get right, it's this. Write a quality book, and you will only have to write it once.

Write a rapid, questionably crafted book, and you will pay for it in edits, reviews, and re-edits if you ever want to write another book again.

Reputation carries you in this industry. In the age of fast-paced, digital entertainment, it's already an uphill battle just to get your books in the hands of the right readers. If their first encounter with your work is a negative one, with a weak story that is littered with grammatical errors, they're not going to read your work again. More than that, they may even tell their friends to avoid you.

However, write a book that removes them from reality and has them glued to the pages until 6am, alarm clock blaring as they begrudgingly step out of bed and head to work, suffering the worst book hangover they've ever experienced...

...they'll buy everything you ever write.

Hell, they may even tell their friends about you.

Take your time and craft a tale that readers will love and

shout about in the streets. Give them the best that you've got. Take your time and pour your soul into the book until you're nothing but an empty husk of what you used to be.

Isn't writing fun?

We're Just Building Sandcastles
Or "The First Draft Mentality"

Contrary to the section above, for your first draft, I want you to forget all of the pressure of writing a book for anyone else but yourself.

It's worth remembering that your book *has* to be good. It's also worth remembering that good comes from process, and we're not all superstars born with golden fingers that can spin stories of perfection on the first outpour.

 The first draft of anything is shit.

— ERNEST HEMINGWAY

Hemingway is a smart guy. He makes some good points. I reckon he'll go far one day.

Watch this space.

As you work through your first draft, understand that everyone writes crap on their first attempt. Remember the first time you tried to ride a bike? Remember your first attempt at baking a Bakewell tart? Remember what it felt like to press the nylons of your six-string and strum your first D chord?

When trying to tell yourself the story, sometimes the words jar. Sometimes the characters misbehave. Sometimes the story untangles from your finely woven net, and you have to spend time wrangling it back in.

There's no one way to write.

Find *your* process. Lose yourself in the sandpit of wordage and get messy. Fight and battle and claw your way toward the end of that first draft until you can hold the digital story in your proverbial hands and shout about it from a metaphorical rooftop.

 I'm simply shoveling sand into a box so that later I can build a sandcastle.

— SHANNON HALE

Focus on the story. Ignore the grammar. Ignore the expectation. Get that first draft done.

There's a reason that books go through rounds and rounds of edits. There's a reason that no one ever shows you the iterations of the iPod. There's a reason that storyboards for films end up in the trash. The creation of art is a constant evolution of friction etched across a grain of sand until you eventually build up enough momentum and drive to spin that grain into a pearl.

Most of all, have fun. Writing can be one of the toughest professions, but if you love the process, then you stand a real chance of finishing that book and making something happen.

A Glass Hammer for a Woollen Nail
Or "The Right Tools to Write"

I won't linger here, because this is really a subject that comes down to personal preference.

You can spend ages finding the right programs to write your book, but in the end, it'll come down to the following:

- Are you actually going to use it? Like, *really* use it?
- Does it allow you to write words?

Microsoft Word, Scrivener, Google Docs, Vellum, Story-Shop, are just a few of the programs that I've played with when writing my books. Mostly now I've settled into a routine of using Scrivener for first drafts, and Microsoft Word for edits—because it works for *me*. Friends of mine swear by solely using Word. Friends of mine swear by working entirely in Google Docs.

Have a play, find what works for you but, realistically, as long as you can write in it, you can create a book.

Perpetual Motion Is a Process
or "Systems, Routines, and Deadlines"

Writing a book is a big task, there's no question about it.

Rarely in our lives are we asked to commit to writing a piece of work that can span upwards of 60,000 words on the lower end of the scale, yet here you are. On the brink of war and about to jump unarmed into the madness.

And guess who's asking you to do it.

You are.

You know what that means, right?

You've only got yourself to hold you accountable.

Which means that, if you let yourself, you can procrastinate. Which means that you *could*, if you allow yourself, leave the work for days at a time and come back to it whenever you want. Which means that no one is telling you to get your ass in the chair and write the words.

Which means your book can take upwards of a few months, to *forever* to write.

It's all down to you.

It's at this point that you may be beginning to freak out. After all, the number of times I tried to write a book in the past and failed because I thought it was too much and I couldn't figure out how to build my own self-discipline process is embarrassing.

However, over time, I came to understand and utilize a few basic principles to help me get started on my book.

And, most importantly, to finish the first draft.

1. Give Yourself a Deadline

Choose a date by which you are going to finish your book.

It could be a month from now, it could be a year. That's up to you and the realities of your life circumstances. Make your deadline realistic. Make it achievable. Give yourself buffer room for the days and weeks where procrastination and life emergencies will inevitably arise.

When I wrote my first full novel (an 80,000-word mind-bending mashup of genres that lives in the bottom drawer of my desk and will never see the light of day again), I set myself the target of completing the book before my next birthday. That gave me a little under three months to write 80,000 words. If I chipped away at it every day, I'd have to have written a little under 1,000 words every day.

That's how *I* made it happen.

You don't have to do it this way.

You could commit to 200 words a day. 100 words a day. Whatever it takes to get you to the end of that first draft.

2. Make Yourself Accountable

Tell people you're writing a book.

Seriously. Tell them. Tell them now, dammit!

It may only be your closest friend, or your mother or father, but tell *someone*. Make yourself accountable. Even just the act of verbalizing to someone else that you're writing your book will infinitely increase your overall motivation. You've put it out there into the world. Now put your money where your mouth is.

3. Become Sacred with Guarding Your Schedule

One of the hardest parts of writing is finding time to commit to the simple act of writing.

We're all busy, there's no denying that. Our worlds are spin-cycles of food regimes, work limitations, and unrequested phone calls with Auntie Doris. Where are we ever going to be able to find the space and time to commit to our writing?

The answer is simple: we have to make it.

Start small. Give yourself a fifteen-minute time slot in the day to write. Tell your children, significant other, parents, friends—whoever—that you are to be undisturbed for fifteen minutes and fifteen minutes only. This period of time will become your sanctuary, your shrine, your holy space of ungodly wonder and homage to the angels of word. Sit your ass in the chair and get to typing.

Stick to this schedule every day (or five days a week, or whatever interval works best for you). The beginning stages may be difficult. You may still get interrupted. But over time you'll train those around you into listening and respecting your space. With clear repetition, you'll prove that this time slot is important to you. You'll earn that sacred space of time, and you'll begin to build your very own word-church, one sexy paragraph at a time.

Fireworks and Champagne!
Or "Celebrating the Wins"

Inevitably, no matter how long it takes you, you will eventually write the two sweetest words in the writer's dictionary.

"The end."

Take a moment.

Pause.

Breathe a sigh of relief.

Sob.

Grab a Kleenex.

Wipe those tears.

Smile.

Beam.

Pump those goddamn fists, because you, my friend, have just written a book.

You.

A book.

Yes.

You.

Hours of toiling in front of a computer screen have yielded a first draft.

Countless nights of tossing and turning, worrying about your plot and your characters have added up to something beautiful.

Immense and indescribable pleasure and pain have culminated in the birth of a word baby, and it is beautiful.

I mean, realistically, probably rough and flawed with errors, but still, *beeeautiful*.

Now's your time to celebrate. You've just completed what 97% of writers who start their journey never complete. You've finished that first draft. You deserve a drink. You deserve a night off. You deserve to gorge on that entire cheesecake you've been eyeing up in the fridge for the last few days but thought you better not because you didn't want to add a millimeter to your waistline—screw what your partner says. You deserve to realize the immensity of the accomplishment laid out before your very eyes.

I'm terrible at celebrating. I often wrap up a first draft and move onto the next thing without pause. Hence why I'm preaching this simple truth to you. Because I don't want you to make the same mistakes I do...

Did...

Sigh... *Do*.

Writing a book is tough. *Finishing* a book is tougher. You've done tremendous things with your words, so take the night off, pop open a bottle of champagne, and let your hair down for one night and one night only.

The hard work continues tomorrow morning.

5

CALLING THE MECHANICS

OR "HOW TO EDIT YOUR BOOK"

\

" *The first draft is black and white. Editing gives the story color.*

— EMMA HILL

E diting is where the true magic of the book happens. It's where that rough coal-like draft morphs into a gleaming diamond. It's where the kinks are worked out of your story. It's where the freshly laid asphalt is smoothed over by the bulldozer.

No one teaches you how to edit a book. And, luckily, that's why we have a fleet of professionals available at our fingertips to do the hard work for us.

It's very easy as writers to get ourselves into a cycle of diminishing returns on our edits. We can spend hours in our isolation chambers combing through our work and tweaking it until we find perfection.

But we'll never find perfection.

My first novella, *Sins of Smoke*, underwent seventeen rounds of edits from just me alone. I re-wrote that sucker word-for-word, trying to tease out any possible improvements and to remove the blemishes.

Would my time have been better spent shipping the work over to an editor?

Absolutely.

Did I think of that at the time?

Shut up, Dan. We'll discuss this in private.

The point is, we can only carry our work so far by ourselves. Eventually we'll need a Samwise Gamgee to drag us the rest of the way. When that time is right is totally up to you but having a professional editor cast their eyes on your work is one of the most powerful ways to actually improve your story, and to make you a better writer.

It may be tough.

You may not like seeing your word baby covered in red scribbles and copious amounts of developmental notes.

But take the constructive feedback, heed the lessons, and you'll grow as an artist. We don't all start as flawless Alice Walkers. We need people to help us along our merry way.

Eggshell, Cream, or Muted Yellow?
Or "Choosing the Right Kind of Editor"

You may be wondering where to begin with finding the right editor for your work. In truth, there are many different types of editor, and they all provide slightly different services depending on your requirements and what stage your book is at. You also may find that you only need to use one or two types of editor, depending on your professional experience and the treatment that your work has already been through before you reach this stage.

Editing is another one of those personal processes where you figure out what works for you. My advice, at the barest of minimums, is to use at least one kind of primary editor, and a proofreader for applying the finishing touches to your work and making it gleam for your reader.

But before we get too ahead of ourselves, here's the lowdown on the types of editors available to you. I've also included an approximate indication of the types of price you may be looking to pay for each edit. These prices are all based on a manuscript of 60,000 words, so feel free to do the math to extrapolate and fit to your own work.[1]

Manuscript Evaluation

Average cost $840

A manuscript evaluation is when an editor provides you with an in-depth letter of feedback of your work. Within the letter, you'll find a full description of the elements of your story that may need improving from a wider, global perspective. These can include criteria such as consistency, plot, structure, characterization, and theme.

Manuscript evaluations are a great way to get an overarching idea of where your story is strong and where it needs work. You won't get a line-by-line review of your book, but you'll understand what's ticking the boxes and what's not from a bird's eye view, which can allow you to go back and self-edit based on these principles.

Developmental Editing

Average cost $1,320

A developmental editor will take a widely holistic view of your book, looking for structural issues, plot holes, and inconsistencies in characterizations. They will also scope out areas for improvement in your writing, including turns of phrase, and particular word choices.

Developmental edits are more comprehensive than a manuscript evaluation, and actually occur within the body of your work, meaning that they will highlight lines and passages directly within your manuscript rather than summarizing in an in-depth letter (though many developmental editors also provide an overarching letter as well as the notes within your text).

Having a developmental edit is a great way to improve your craft as a writer. You may be overwhelmed by the number of notes and edits within your work but know that this is not unusual. Every writer—both amateur and seasoned—is met with a document covered in red squiggles after a developmental edit. It's part and parcel of the job.

Copy-Editing

Average cost $960

This is a comprehensive look at your writing under the microscope. Copy editors will ensure that your writing is tight on a sentence-level, focusing on grammar, spelling, fact-checking, punctuation, and correct word-usage.

This kind of edit is a lot more granular and will bring your work into a specific "house-style" so that your work is consistent and clean throughout. For many writers, copy edits are a staple of their editing journey.

Beta Readers

While beta readers shouldn't necessarily be considered editors, many authors benefit from utilizing a small group of early readers to help give them an idea of how their larger reader base will react to a story.

Beta readers are often super fans who will provide constructive, critical feedback from a reader's perspective. Mostly, they're looking at the story as a whole. If you write in a series, beta readers are a great way to check for consistency and to pick up on any loose threads you may have missed when you got stuck in the weeds of drafting.

> **PRO TIP:** Be selective with changes that beta readers ask you to make. Ensure they will actually benefit the story as a whole and not just serve one individual's preferences.

You also don't have to use beta readers at all. For me, I find that beta readers provide a good gauge as to whether a story is delivering what I want to deliver to the right readers.

To find beta readers, raid your networks. Put out shouts on social media or content your reader base (even if it's only tiny). Beta teams are generally rather intimate, so a handful should serve you well.

Proofreading

Average cost $600

This is your final sweep for lingering errors. Proofreaders focus on the fluidity of the read, taking note of typos, inconsistencies, formatting errors, and missing pieces.

> **PRO TIP:** No matter what you're publishing and when, ensure that your book always passes through this final, critical round of edits. It could make the difference between raving reviews, and a slew of negatives.

Choosing the right kind of edits for your book is entirely up to you. What you will find is that, after receiving your edits from your editor, there will be more work for you to complete upon their receipt.

After you receive a round of edits, take your time absorbing the comments, and then put them into action. Every time you sweep through your manuscript, you should be creating a stronger, better project. That lump of coal that you hacked away at in your private mineshaft is getting closer and closer to becoming the fabled diamond that we spoke of.

And, oh, isn't that something exciting.

Voila!

Once your edits are done, and your proofreader has performed their final sweep...

Don't touch it!

Put it down.

Now.

No playing, Timmy. I said leave it alone!

The proofreader's work should be the final touch of your book. A proofreader should catch every last error that remains (though, let's be honest, we're all human, and *no* process is fool proof). Anything you do to the book from then on will not only potentially introduce new errors, but it will also have wasted your money in hiring a proofreader.

So, leave it.

Stare at it in disbelief.

Celebrate again!

You have done it.

We are here.

With a *finished* book.

On your screen.

A book that is shaped and ready to be delivered to the world.

A book that will bear your name on its cover and will be read by readers—real-life people—in the very near future.

Give yourself a pat on the back.

Pound down that chardonnay.

Then let's get crackin' on the next step.

----

1. Source: "How Much Does It Cost to Self-Publish a Book in 2021?" (https://blog.reedsy.com/cost-to-self-publish-a-book/)

6

THE FIDDLY BITS

OR "FRONT AND BACK MATTER"

I almost didn't include this section.

But then I realized, no book I've personally ever read has covered this element of publishing, and it's one that gave me a lot of headaches when I first dipped my toes into the publishing pool.

It was an inky pool. Very black. Very sticky. I should have dipped my quill first.

That wasn't a euphemism.

The "front matter" and the "back matter" simply refers to those extra few pages and sections that pad your story. They're the parts that you've likely glossed over in the past in your feverish efforts to get your nose stuck into the book.

Front and back matter includes items like the copyright page, the dedication, the afterwords, and the "also by" pages. When done properly, well-chosen and well-formatted front and back matter will help readers distinguish your carefully crafted, professional-looking, self-published book from the others on the shelf who have half-assed their efforts and skipped over this entirely.

Although we don't necessarily always read the pages of seemingly useless information at the beginning of the books we read, we know they need to be there. It's a part of the reader experience. We don't go to the movies to watch the commercials, but we accept that that's how the format runs. It's the same with books. Before you get to the body of the story, you have to flick past the copyright page, the dedications, and whatever else the authors have thrown in there.

It's all part of the fun.

At the end of the book we, as readers, expect to find certain pages. We expect links and suggestions of the authors' other works, as well as a thank you to the people who have helped make the book possible.

Each publisher has their own preference over what they include and exclude in the front and back matter of the books and, as always, there is no right or wrong way to determine your list. Some of the pages are fundamental staples of particular books, others are just preferences.

Here's a look at some of the most commonly included elements you may choose to include before and after the main content of your book.

Front Matter
The Stuff Before the Story

Praise and quotes: Many traditionally published books will feature an opening page of critical and peer reviews, showcasing the best of the best of the praise that others have sung about the book. This is more common in physical print books, considering readers will immediately see the hype just by flicking to the first page.

. . .

Title page: A single, clean page that showcases the title of your book. This features the author's name and will often have the publisher's logo present, too.

Other titles by: This is a page to list all of your other works, if you have any. If you don't yet, you may want to skip this one.

Copyright: Your copyright page will show readers and authors alike the core information that protects your book's content from being stolen or plagiarized. You can find standard templates for copyright pages online, with most featuring the year of publication of the book, the publisher information, and details about how the book may be used by the reader. Some authors also stick cover designer information and editor contact details to help support those who have helped them make the book a reality.

Dedication: These are generally pretty short, one- or two-line sentences to give thanks to someone special in the author's life. My dedications in the past have been made to family members and friends as a tribute for the role they have played in my life.

Keep these short and sweet, please. No one wants a three-page Oscars speech where the music is forced to start playing and a weeping actor is dragged from stage.

Epigraph: Some authors (like myself) like to go all fancy and include a meaningful quote toward the beginning of their book. This could be a song verse, a stanza from a poem, or a single line quote that informs the rest of the book and sets the tone of the story you are about to tell.

Contents page: Your contents page lists the chapter numbers and titles, as well as the page numbers of each section for your print readers. In eBook form, these chapters will be hyperlinked for the reader's convenience, allowing them to tap the screen and go straight to where they'd like to go.

Foreword: A foreword is typically written by another author on your behalf, preferably within your genre. It provides a short introduction to the book from someone else's perspective, providing excitement and social proof of your book's message for the reader.

Half-title: A minimalist page with the book title repeated to close off the front matter of your book before the main body of the text.

Back Matter
After the Story Is Over

Afterword: An afterword is a concluding segment of the book, usually written from a different perspective or time and, similarly to the foreword, will often be written by someone other than the author. It is rare to see both a foreword and an afterword in a book, typically because they serve a similar purpose. An afterword is more commonly used in reprints of books to tell the narrative of how the book has changed over time, its cultural significance, and the impact it has had on its readers.

Author notes: These are your chance to connect with the reader once the book is finished.

When done well, author notes provide a real, emotional connection between reader and author, often granting the reader a glimpse inside the author's life. I've seen author notes that describe the author's perspective as they finish the last edits of their books, I've seen authors describe their latest holidays and share information on how that's informing their next book, I've seen authors give behind-the-scenes glimpses into how the book the reader is currently holding came to be, where the idea came from, why they chose to write *that* story, and any struggles they've faced along the way.

Those are my favorites.

Whatever you choose to write about, if you do choose to write author notes, the more personal you can make them, the easier it will be for readers to buy into *you* as an author and potentially pick up that next book.

Mailing list sign-up page: I always make sure to include a link for readers to sign up to my mailing list as close to the end of the book as possible. I offer a free novella for anyone who provides their email and joins my list, and that works pretty well for me. It enables me to not lose the reader once they've finished my book, and I can keep in touch with them over the years whenever I have news on releases or just generally want to check in.

Promotional slot: There's no hard and fast rule to how many of these you can put into your book. If you've got other books you'd like your readers to be aware of, and you want to give them more clout, include a dedicated page to that book. If it's in the same genre and style as the current book your reader is holding, they may be likely to pick it up straight away.

> **PRO TIP:** Don't go crazy. Choose one or two things to advertise, and then move on. If you load the back of your books with dozens of things your reader should do, they'll do none of them.

Acknowledgements: This section allows you to highlight those who have helped this book come to life. While the dedication page is typically only a brief line or two, authors can make full use of the acknowledgements to thank their mother, brother, sister, loved one, friends, colleagues, whoever you fancy throwing recognition to before the curtain closes and that big ol' hook comes for you.

About the author: This is your professional author bio. Sometimes accompanied with a picture of yourself, this gives the reader an overview of you as an author and what you do.

. . .

Other titles by: Often repeated at the beginning and end of the book, this is your final reminder to the reader of the other works you've published. If you're a publisher with works from other authors in the same genre, you may want to use this space to promote similar works from other authors that the reader may enjoy.

But, Which Ones Should I Use?

What you may notice is that the above items listed are not in alphabetical order. This is because I've placed them in an order that will typically be found inside the books.

The order matters. I don't know why, and I don't know who made the order, but it does. It's the same reason my mama doesn't allow me to eat dessert before I've finished my chicken. I mean, historically there *is* a reason to the order you eat your food (you don't want to fill your tummy with empty calories so that you're too full for the nutritious stuff—just in case you didn't know), but I'll give you the same answer that mother gave me: "You want a reason? Fine. Here it is. 'Just because.'"

Thanks, Mama. Real helpful.

If you pick up any book on your shelf, you'll notice the likenesses inside each one. There may be a few irregularities, but for the most part, the order listed above is what you'll find.

Take and leave the sections that you wish to include. Some sections, such as the copyright and title pages, are fundamental to every book. But others, such as the foreword, afterword, or epigraph won't be in every novel or guide you hold in your hands. Get familiar with what the books you love use and decide what you're happy to include.

This is *your* book, after all.

7

A PRETTY PACKAGE WITH A BOW ON TOP

OR "SOURCING A KILLER BOOK COVER"

> *Why would they have book covers if we aren't supposed to judge the book by them? It makes no sense.*
>
> — INGRID WEIR

Your book's cover can be the make or break between a book that is picked up and read, and a book that is ignored.

We've all heard the old adage, "You shouldn't judge a book by its cover," but unfortunately, I'm here to tell you that doesn't apply in the self-publishing arena. With literally millions of books in the Amazon, Kobo, and Google charts, and thousands more uploaded daily, you have to pull out all the stops to ensure that your book catches the eye of the readers you want to buy your work.

> *Good cover design is not only about beauty... it's a visual sales pitch. It's your first contact with a potential reader. Your cover only has around 3 seconds to catch a browsing reader's attention. You want to stand out and make them pause and consider, and read the synopsis.*

— EEVA LANCASTER

There's a reason why peacocks flash their plumage to their mates. There's a reason that your eye is drawn to the gleaming yellow Lamborghini over the rusty brown Volvo. The human brain is attracted to the pretty, the different, and the shiny. When browsing through a digital storefront littered with books and their covers, your eye will inevitably be drawn to certain book covers over others.

It's not always about pretty colors either (though, often it helps). It's about the layout, the choice of font used for the title, it's the characters featured on the jacket, even the word choice of the title itself could make all the difference between a book that is clicked so furiously that readers develop RSI in their finger, and a book that is scrolled straight past. I mean, imagine if *The Hunger Games* had a totally different title and cover. Would you really want to read a book called, "I'm a Hungry Volunteer, Get Me Out of Here"?

The point is that as much as we'd like to believe that our words can stand on their own merit, it's just not true. And if you want to reach the right readers, you need to ensure that you package your gleaming triumph in as pretty a cover as possible.

With a bow on top.

Maybe some glitter, too.

But how the hell do you go about finding a cover designer who will not only deliver you an amazing book cover for your work, but will help you stand out from the crowd? Where do you even begin?

Well, as always, my friend, the work starts with *you*.

The Best of the Same but Different
Or "Genre Tropes for Book Covers"

Before you even think about finding a cover designer, you have to be confident that you know what you want them to create.

In Chapter 3 we looked at the concept of genre tropes. The same rules apply here. Browse through the top 100 in the charts of your favorite genre and you'll begin to notice something of a trend—a commonality, if you will.

Take post-apocalyptic books, for example. Over the last half a decade there has been a trend in how a post-apocalyptic book cover *should* look. Scan the charts and you will find dozens of book covers featuring one or two characters silhouetted, facing away from the reader, walking toward the post-apocalyptic landscape they find themselves thrown in. There'll be broken buildings, there'll be mushroom clouds, storms, and you can almost guarantee there'll be some form of dog or rifle featured in there somewhere. (Who doesn't love a good pooch in their stories?) The titles will often be written in a bold, cracked, sans serif font (without the little embellishes found in a font like Times New Roman), and the only thing that may vary will be the color choices.

That's the standard. That's what designers are creating, and that's what's selling the books.

"But don't all the book covers look the same?"

In a sense, yes. In a way, no.

Readers want the same, but different.

Take a look at the following examples of current post-apocalyptic books that are trending in the charts, and tell me that they're exactly the same.

Left to right: "Dead South," by Zach Bohannon, "They Rot," by Luke Kondor and Daniel Willcocks (Credit: J Caleb Design), and "Wizard of the Wasteland," by Jon Cronshaw (Credit: Yocla Designs)

The point is, genre tropes very much apply to book designers, too.

When you begin to source your cover designer, you'll notice that the designers that are *crushing* it for authors specialize in book covers and book covers alone. They're not spending their hours creating digital product mock-ups of china pots or managing painstakingly careful strokes on a canvas to create an abstract piece that portrays the emotion of joy.

There's a different science associated with cover design. There's a psychology. There's a specificity. Your readers expect a certain type of book and that begins with the cover. Your cover designer will also likely specialize in a particular *genre* and will therefore know the difference between a book cover that grabs the attention of *your* reader, and a book cover that gets lost amongst the muck.

"But isn't art about bending the rules? Won't something *completely* different stand out more?"

Again... In a sense, yes. In a way, no.

When it comes to bending the rules and trendsetting a new direction in cover art, traditional publishing houses still rule the roost. There's a lot that traditional publishers can get away with considering that they have a fleet of businesses, bookstores, and marketing channels at their fingertips. Traditional publishers benefit from the fact that they have immense financial backing, reputational standing, and their physical distribution channels. HarperCollins could literally put out a book with a blank white cover and it would move thousands of copies simply for the fact that they can get that book under people's noses.

You, however, are a business of one, which means that unfortunately you have to play by some of the rules of the independent market in order to make sure that your book is seen.

Can you bend the rules?

Yes.

Should you bend the rules?

Maybe.

I'm not saying that it is impossible to create a unique piece of art that will stand as a book cover and move copies of your book. What I am saying is that this is a game of odds, and to increase your odds of success there are fundamental rules that you should play by—particularly in the earlier stages of your career.

Take some time now to explore the charts of your chosen bookstore.

Browse *your* chosen genre and get familiar with *those* book covers.

Take note of particular color choices. Write down anything that catches your eye. Document any distinguishing features that you see repeated across the spectrum of covers. Familiarize yourself with the expectations that the reader has of the covers that sell. Make sure you have some kind of note-taking app where you can keep a record of the images you like. Build a collection of the covers that appeal to you and you'll be able to use this as a reference later when putting together a design brief for your cover designer of choice.

Avengers... Assemble!
Or "Researching and Contacting Designers"

There are a plethora of cover designers waiting for you to approach them on the internet, sitting behind a computer screen, anxiously awaiting your email to set them free on the digital canvas so they can create a masterpiece for your work.

So, how do you find the *right* cover designer for your book?

Over the last ten years, an increasing number of cover designers have poked their heads up out of the ground and made themselves visible for the ever-increasing raft of indie publishers who are unleashing their work out on the market.

Just a rudimentary search on Google will greet you with dozens and dozens of results of possible cover designers who are all vying to become the artist for your book cover.

But what is it that separates the good from the bad from the ugly?

There's no easy way to answer this question. Some covers designers can produce amazing pieces of work for their clients. If you can create a flawless design brief, you can maximize your chances of success. However, there are a myriad of other factors which may prevent you from getting a great cover, even with a great design brief.

Here are just a few tips that I personally use when seeking out a new cover designer:

Seek recommendations: Speak to other writers that you may know who have had cover designs.

It's the simplest route, but one that will benefit you greatly. With recommendations, you have social proof that the cover designer delivers what is asked for. You have examples of their art, you can question their process. Word of mouth is powerful, my friend.

There are a number of easy ways you can find recommendations.

- Ask your writer friends
- Put out a call on a social media or on a writers' forum asking for recommendations
- Use the "Look Inside" feature of Amazon to view the copyright page of a book you like the look of, sometimes (though not always) the artist is credited there

Send a tester email: You can tell a lot from a cover designer by the way that they reply to their emails.

When working with a new cover designer, I will often send over a short email asking what their current availability is (no point sourcing designers who are going to take nine months to complete a design I need for three months' time). I might also ask whether they have any specifics in terms of the design brief that they wish to receive from a client. Use these small, legitimate, probing questions to form a connection.

Sometimes you may find that a designer will take a week to get back to you. Sometimes you will find that they will take a day. Sometimes it may take a month.

When you receive your reply, take a second to examine the tone of the designer's response.

Do they sound friendly?

Are they professional?

Are they answering your questions in a way that feels as if they're not rushing you along?

All of these will be important when it comes to your design as it's not always just about the end product of your book cover. Communication is fundamental when working with a cover designer, and if you can't even start off on the right foot with a decent email exchange then you're already setting yourself up for problems later down the line when you start actually talking shop about your design.

A good cover designer should help guide you through their process so that they deliver the best possible product they can.

After all, book covers aren't cheap—at least not the good ones, anyway.

Picking Up the Pieces
Or "Pre-made Covers"

If you're not looking to pay a fair mint, there are budget alternatives out there.

Pre-made covers are book covers that have been commissioned, but the commissioning author has chosen not to take them. Often, designers will provide two or three variants of a cover for an author to choose from. One of those covers will be chosen, the rest will be cast asunder.

But designers are smart. They know that the other covers are good, and therefore they auction these covers to authors who wish to pay less for a cover. Pre-made covers aren't fully customizable, but you can request your book title and your author name to be featured on the book.

This is a fantastic way to save money, while ensuring you get a quality design. There is a whole raft of websites out there from which you can buy pre-mades. You'll find that some are certainly better than others, but all of these sites have a portfolio page where you can scan for a cover that appeals to you, and then add your information to its front.

Of course, your cover may not completely fit the requirements you're after with this method, but you can get somewhat close if you hunt around. Once a pre-made is sold to you, most sites also take that design off the market, so you know that you're the only one with that shiny book cover, too.

Sandrine! Crack Open the Piggy Bank!
Or "How Much Do Covers Cost?"

Cover design can be as pricy or as cheap as you want it to be, ranging anywhere from $50 to $2,000 depending on the reputation of your designer and the work they produce.

Based on the covers that I have received and the price range that I have seen from friends' work, I would suggest that a good price to pay for a custom book cover is anywhere in the region from $250 to $500. Most of my own covers have been in the region of $350 on average and you could definitely get some good quality work for that price range.

Credit Card, Cheque, or Cash?
Or "How Does Payment Work?"

There are a few options when it comes to paying for your cover.

- **Payment up front:** Nice and easy. Pay up front. Get the money side of things out of the way and get going with your cover design.
- **Deposit first:** Pay a small percentage ahead of the actual design process, then secure your commission by paying the remaining fee at the end. Deposits can vary, but shouldn't exceed 50% up front.
- **Payment upon delivery:** Less common, but some designers are happy to go through the work ahead of payment.

I've worked with designers who have dabbled in all of these pricing structures and have found that the process has always been smooth and frictionless.

Depending on your constitution, you may find that you

prefer not to pay a penny until you have something that you're happy with. If you're more trusting, you may be happy paying the amount up front. I would always advise to read the small print on the designers' sites to find out how payment works if there is ever a dispute. The last thing you want is for a designer to take your money up front and then ghost you for twelve months. If you've followed the steps so far, that should never happen to you.

No Ikea Instructions, Please
Or "Creating Your Design Brief"

Communicating with cover designers can be a whole new language to some. We've all been hit with mental blocks when trying to describe what we like about a particular piece of art. We use phrases like, "It just needs a little bit more *oomph*," "It just isn't *speaking* to me," or "What if it just had a bit more, you know, that kind of... Like... It feels like it's missing something... Not sure what... But, yeah. That."

There's an easy way to get around all of these problems. Designers speak in very visual terms, therefore, *show* them the visuals.

When I'm piecing together a cover brief, I will always be sure to throw in lots and lots of examples of the type of thing that I'm looking for from the visuals. I will provide a design brief filled with tangible examples that all share some kind of commonality of the book cover that I am trying to create for my work.

This means finding the things that books have in common (remember that list of book covers you made... Now's a good time to use that).

For example, if I'm commissioning a cover for a romance

book that's going to sit nicely in the charts amongst its brothers and sisters, I might find examples of books with couples embracing on the cover, maybe a little pink hue around the image in order to give the feeling of "love," and possibly some variations of a cursive font for the title text.

What I *won't* do is mix the images you've already provided with something entirely different. Your images of couples staring into the sunset won't often mix well with covers that show an amalgam of swirling text, candy hearts, and illustrated flowers.

You may *love* both kinds of covers, but you're only commissioning one. Don't confuse the designer. Pick one and run with it.

Make it easy for the designer to design the piece that you want. Although designers are experts in what they do, they cannot read your mind. Therefore, make your mind an open book and give them the information that they require, as accurately as possible, as specific as possible, and they will make the cover you need.

After all, no one knows your book like you do.

It is worth noting that many cover designers supply their own design briefs in order to ease newcomers into the commission process. Some designers know exactly what it is they want to extract from the author and therefore all you need to do is complete the sheets to the best of your ability. Others allow for a bit more flexibility and let you take the lead with your commission.

If you're sitting there with your knees knocking, fingernails chewed to the quick because this all seems rather overwhelming and out of your comfort zone, don't worry. I've got you covered.

A good cover design brief can be broken down into a few key components.

1. Book Information

Your book's information is simply a basic text list of the information you want featured on the book as well as the genre in which your book is hoping to fit.

Be sure to include:

- Your book title
- Your author name
- Your series title (if you have one)
- Your book's tagline (optional)
- Your genre
- Any quotes from other writers or any additional other information you wish to see

Ensure that everything is spelled correctly. It is not the designer's job to proofread your work, it is the designer's job to copy and paste the information, verbatim, on to your book cover.

Featuring this information at the top of your brief is incredibly useful for the designer as it's just an easy way for them to access the information that they need when attacking that design.

2. A Summary of the Book

I will always ensure that I have included a summary of the book and what I am trying to achieve with the story.

If I'm re-covering a book because the last cover is tired or isn't converting well, I will also feature this somewhere near the top of the brief to show a little bit of the history of the book. I will also include a much more holistic overview of what the story is about and some of the key events that take place that might influence the composition of the characters and the design of the front.

If you're writing in a series, be sure to tell the designer this so that your upcoming cover will fit with the other books in that narrative.

Your overview is really just your chance to set the scene and bring the designer into your world and help them understand your story. Remember, they don't know you and your journey. They deal with hundreds of writers a year. Give them context to quickly help them absorb who you are and what this book is about.

This isn't a blurb, which generally gives a brief overview of your story and is aimed at a reader. Here you can be more conversational and in-depth, finding your optimum way to communicate what your book is, how the cover can communicate the story, and any particular emotional tone that you might want to capture with the art.

3. The Feel

This is the part of the brief in which I image dump.

Take those covers you found that you love and drop them onto the page. I tend to prioritize the images, grading them as I go so the designer can see where my head is at. I create a top row of my preferred choices, I have a middle line which showcases more of the general themes and advises on the composition of the design, and at the bottom I throw in a few more examples of book covers that I like that still fit with the general theme but are a little bit more on the cusp of where I feel the design should be. This allows the designer a little bit of flexibility to stretch their creative muscles and produce something that reflects what I'm after but which also showcases their artistic talents in the most effective way possible.

For me, this is the fun part as you begin to see your cover unfold. It's where you really get to narrow down and zero in on the type of cover that your designer will be presenting to you. The more specific you can get, the more targeted you are, the more direction you give, the greater the chance of the designer delivering a version of what you envisaged in your mind.

4. Main Character Traits and Features

This section I reserve for anything specific to my story that I feel needs to go on the cover.

In my most recent cover brief for my apocalyptic serial, "When Winter Comes," I made sure to specify the age of the boy and girl that feature on the cover. I also provided a little bit of guidance in terms of what I *don't* want to see on the cover. Since post-apocalyptic covers generally feature firearms of some sort, and my main characters don't carry them, I wanted to ensure that the artist knew not to default to a cover that is specifically military in tone.

If there is anything specific that you'd like to see from your cover, that is, a particular style of cutlass, a rare breed of flower, a paranormal sigil, or even something as abstract as a purple carrot that hovers over the top of a dog's head in the same way that Sparx the Dragonfly used to follow Spyro the Dragon, then now is a good time to note that down so that it gets included.

5. Book Blurb

Your book blurb is your sales pitch to your reader. It's the short paragraph or two that you see on the back of a paperback, or on the sales page of your chosen online book store.

If you haven't yet created your book blurb, then now would be a great time to do so. If you're having your paperback commissioned, it helps your artist not only to get more of an idea of the tone of the book, but they can also start building the back cover for you.

See Me After Class
Or "Reviewing Your Designs"

Once you have agreed your design brief and the artist has asked any final questions that they may have, it's time to play the waiting game.

How long does this take?

It depends entirely on the designer and the expectations that you've set together. A good cover designer should be able to give you an expected delivery date and deliver upon that. If they hit any complications along the way, they should be able to at least let you know in advance of any changes to your schedule.

Remember: You are the customer.

You are paying their fee.

If they can't deliver upon what they've promised, you are well within your rights to speak up and find out what's going on.

I've had a pretty good streak with cover designers, and I put that mostly down to clear, honest communication. I always ensure that the designer has a good reputation, and that way I don't get burned. You may think you've found a cheap cover designer that can deliver all you want and more, but is it really worth it if they're going to spend three months longer than you've planned and what they return would be better placed on the bathroom wall of a gas station off the I-95?

Step down off your soap box, Dan. You promised to talk about reviewing the art.

Of course, Other Dan.

Sooner or later, your designer will hand you back your book cover design. Often, designers will take the time to provide two or three "concepts" of what the design could look like.

These are *not* final designs.

They may be beautiful, and they may look polished and perfect and everything you ever hoped for, but they are *not* final.

I've been there, trust me. I still get those butterflies of excitement whenever I see the first iteration of a cover for my work. The designer will always be keen to sign off the art straight away, because in doing so they can move on and claim the money you promised to pay them (depending on how you've handled your financial arrangement).

Something strange happens in the human mind when you see a pretty picture. You get blinded by that keenness and you can't think of anything that you want to change.

It's perfect.

They were perfect.

You're perfect.

But in the immortal words of the legendary, five-piece, super girl group, the *Spice Girls*, "Stop right now."

Take a breath.

Reply to your designer to tell them that you like what

you see so far, but you need some time to let the art sink in and to find any possible tweaks. I often tell designers that I'll get back to them in a couple of days.

Why do I do this?

Because once the excitement grinds down to a low simmer, you begin to notice the things that your eager mind was too blind to see. The blood dripping off the lettering just isn't hitting you right. The shade of green they've used is a little too bright and detracts from the houses in the background. There are a couple of pixels in a different color to the rest. That shadowy figure on the front doesn't quite represent the characters I've chosen for my book.

It happens.

We need time to process things. And when you're spending upward of $300 on a book cover, you want to make sure you get things right. A lot of designers bake in "unlimited revisions" to their processes. Make use of them—but don't abuse them. Designers are people too, with time and patience limits and they deserve for you to be as fair to them as you want them to be to you.

> **PRO TIP:** Your book cover will need to stand out on an online sales page. Often your cover will be reduced to a thumbnail on your screen. Whenever I get a new cover, I will reduce the image to the same size as those on the online charts I want my book to compete in. Does it stand out against the rest? Does it catch my eye? If not, why? All of this is good feedback for your designer.

Can You Make it "Pop" a Little More?

Or "How to Give Useful Feedback"

"Make it pop more," is not useful feedback for a designer.

"Something just feels a little... off?" is not useful feedback for a designer.

"Can you make it a little more horror-y," is not useful feedback for a designer.

Speaking the language of art is a difficult skill to learn. However, there are some tips to help you get across what you're trying to communicate without sounding like you're a background character in a Dr. Suess film.

- **Be visual:** If you're struggling to *write* the problem, then *image* the problem. Take pictures of your cover concept, draw lines on the printed sheet, find tangible examples of other covers that have delivered the effect you're trying to go for. Help the designer *see* what you want them to see.

- **Get feedback from others:** Get feedback from your readers, ask your writerly friends what they think, see if you've got a friend who's pretty artsy who may be able to communicate what it is you're trying to communicate. (Caveat, ensure the people you are asking are actually involved in the book world and understand cover design on some level. Your cousin with her C-grade A-level may have some idea of what good lighting and composition can do to an image, but cover design is its own form of science. You wouldn't ask a car mechanic to diagnose the problems with your B-52 jet engine, would you? My recommendation would be to stick to other authors who write specifically within *your* genre. They're who you're trying to reach.)

- **Be respectful, be honest:** If you're not sure why your cover isn't resonating with you in the right way, or if you can't quite put into words what the problem is, just tell the designer. See if you can arrange a call with them to talk it through. Be transparent and tell them that you need help verbalizing the issue. Maybe they can help you directly. A good cover designer should *want* to please their customer. After all, that's how they ensure repeat business.

The Point of Diminishing Returns
Or "When You Should Let it Go"

There's a limit to how many rounds of amends is useful, and there comes a time when your opinion becomes damaging to the overall design of your cover.

It's a tough balance to strike. The artist is (or should be) the professional. They know what sells, they research their covers, they know the ins and outs of how to speak to a reader through cover art. However, you have your ideas in your head, and you want to pay for something that you're proud of.

There's no accurate way to tell where the middle ground lays in the design. For me, I ensure that I am happy with all of the *specifics* of the image and generally try to trust that the designer has done everything they can to create a powerful cover image. I'll pick up on tweaks with the fonts, I'll ensure the characters are representative of my work, and I'll ask for a little bit more blood or shade or darkness where I feel it is appropriate.

And I'll end it there.

You could circle the drain forever with amends and updates, and all you're going to end up with is an image that has lost all of its professional designer influence and all you'll be left with is a piece of custom art, not a book cover.

I've seen many authors spinning around in endless loops with an ever-increasingly-pissed-off designer who, no matter how hard they try, can't please their customer. I'd advise a *maximum* of three or four rounds of amends with the designer before you're done.

Finito.

Fini.

If you can't communicate what you want with four email or phone exchanges, you're not going to be able to communicate what you want or need at all, or you shouldn't have approached your designer in the first place.

This is why we research.

Treat your designer with respect. They're still people. Just because they state unlimited revisions, doesn't mean they'll be happy at round 463 of edits where their beautifully crafted cover has become nothing more than a cross between the Mona Lisa and Dali's Clocks.

Four revisions. Max. Then walk away.

That'll do, pig. That'll do.

Pens Down, Thumbs Up!
Or "Finalizing Your Design"

Once you're happy with your design, finalize it.

You're done, kid. You've got a brand-spanking new, shiny book cover.

For me, this may just be my favorite part of the process. It's the moment where you can finally see how your book will stack up against the others on the digital stores. It's the part where everything starts falling into place and you feel like you have a "real" book in your hands.

Thank your cover designer. I mean it. Send them a hearty thanks and let them know they did a good job. If you ever want to use them again in the future, they'll remember you favorably and will be more likely to find a way to squeeze you into their schedule.

And there you have it. One fit-for-purpose, dazzling book cover.

As always, celebrate. Pat yourself on the back. Show the cover off to your friends and family. Be proud of what you've created.

But! Do not release this cover out into the wild yet.

Your book cover is one of your greatest promotional tools. Too often authors are eager to show off their book covers months, even years ahead of their launch. For the maximum impact with your cover, work a cover reveal into your marketing strategy (see Chapter 10). You only get one chance to make a good impression, so don't waste it by hurling that puppy on your social platforms ahead of time.

We'll get to all of that shortly. For now, ensure that your designer has sent you everything you need. Different storefronts require slightly different sizing for their eBook cover art. You may find you get sent two or three slight variations of cover size. This is normal. Your designer should know which fits best. If you're unsure, simply check out your chosen platform of choice and they should state their cover size in their setup page.

PRO TIP: Where possible, ask your designer to provide you with the "source files" for your cover. These files contain all the design information (fonts, colors, images, layers etc) so that if you ever lose contact with your cover designer, you can easily hand this file to a new designer to tweak and amend later. This is also incredibly useful if you have a particular brand and design for your series. There is usually a charge of up to $50 to claim the source files, but this will cover you in the long term.

What Comes Next?

Well, you've prettified the outside of your book. It's time to prettify the inside.

8

IT'S WHAT'S ON THE INSIDE THAT COUNTS

OR "FORMATTING AND TYPESETTING"

Jump back half a decade, and the word "formatting" was enough to induce fearful fits of sleepless nights and pounding heads. Authors working on a shoestring budget (myself included) could spend hours lost in the hidden functions and tools of Microsoft Word in order to find the perfect way to lay out their books on the page. Some authors wiled away their time in Adobe's InDesign, some in Microsoft Publisher, but no matter what tools you used, one thing was always as clear as day:

Formatting a book was a nightmare bitch of colossal proportions.

Luckily for *you*, however, all that has changed.

There are a great number of ways to format your book and make it look as professional as the books published by the traditional houses. Some of these options are pricier than others, so you can weave and adapt your methods depending on your budget.

No matter which you choose, ensure that you're prioritizing the reader experience and making it as easy as possible for them to enjoy your story.

"But, what are the options?" I hear you scream.

Allow me to illuminate the possibilities.

1. Learn How to Format Your Own Book

Yes! You *can* format your own book.

Should you?

Well, that's a question that only you can answer.

It's possible to create a professionally laid-out book with something as simple as Microsoft Word. I've done it. I was proud of the result.

Was it easy?

No.

Did it take up a lot of time to learn and tweak each file?

Yes. Would that time have been better spent elsewhere?

Maybe.

Did I save any money?

A tonne.

Bear in mind that this was between 2015 and 2017, and there were no real alternatives out there that wouldn't have me cutting holes in my pocket to look for the loose change in the lost universes hidden between the threads. Formatting gained a reputation as an expensive service, and I wasn't in a position to pay that kind of money.

So, I learned.

Like anything in life, it's easy when you know how, but it did come with its own complications. Often there would be hidden formatting instructions in the file that would take me hours to seek and tweak, uploading files to the publishing platforms took ages just to test that everything had worked okay, and I may have lost more hair in that three-day period of finalizing my first book than I care to admit.

The point is, that you *can* learn to format a book. If you're handy with tech and design, maybe this is a good route for you. However, learning involves a considerable investment of time, and would that time be better spent working on your next book, or sorting out your launch plan?

Only you can decide.

2. Hire a Formatter

Luckily for you, you're joining the era of self-publishing where there are many authors and creatives who *have* learned how to format books that will look polished and professional on Amazon, Kobo, Google, and all the other platforms.

A quick Google search will glean results of professionals who are more than happy to take your book and give it a professional format. Many cover designers offer this as part of their package, and if you're searching on a shoestring budget, marketplaces like Fiverr can offer a less expensive way to quickly turn that messy Word document into a publishable file.

How much does it cost to hire a formatter? According to Reedsy's 2021 blog post, "48% of people pay less than $500," and "30% of people pay $500–$1,000" for their book formatting.

3. Format your book with Vellum

$249.99 paperbacks & ebooks / $199.99 ebooks only

Vellum has saved me countless hours and dollars on formatting my book.

It's not the cheapest way to get your start in publishing, at $249.99 for the fully licensed program, the up-front costs may be enough to sway you toward alternate methods. In my experience, if you're going to be in this for the long haul, Vellum is worth every penny.

What used to take me hours of formatting and tweaking now takes 10–15 minutes, at the most. Vellum is built for self-publishers, by self-publishers, and features an array of built-in design options to make your book unique and professional.

Simply upload your document into Vellum and play around with the design. Once you're happy, a simple click of a button will generate all the files you need to upload your book to all of the major platforms.

If you're only looking at publishing eBooks, you can purchase the cheaper option at $199.99, but in my opinion the additional $50 is money well-spent. Vellum is a one-time purchase, and then you can make as many books as you want. I have far out-earned anything that I would have previously spent on formatting both in terms of time and money, just by using this program.

PRO TIP: Vellum is, unfortunately, exclusive to Mac users and is unavailable on PC. However, you can access Vellum through a MacInCloud which is a paid service that allows you to access the Mac OS on Windows machines.

4. Other Available Online Services to Format Your Book

If all of these options sound too expensive or time-wieldy for you, then there are a few free alternatives out there to help you get your book into a shape that you'll be happy with.

Among the few reputable online formatters are:

- Amazon's "**Kindle Create**"
- PublishDrive's **"Ebook Converter"**
- Reedsy's **"Write A Book"**

All of these online services will allow you to upload your document and arrange your book in a way that looks clean and professional. Better yet, they're all free to use!

Of course, free software will always have its limitations. But if you're looking for a clean, simple polish for your books, this may be a good place for you to start.

I Can't Listen to a Newspaper
Or "The Right Formats"

So, you have your book formatted, but how do you know what files are needed to export the books to the right platforms?

You have three primary options available when you export a file, and the type of file you need will largely depend upon the platform you are choosing to publish your book on.

- **Amazon's KDP:** For the best result when uploading your book to Amazon, you will need an ".epub" or a ".KPF" file. ".DocX" files *can* work, but I would always recommend an ".epub" file for ease of use. While Amazon used to accept

".mobi" files, these are no longer acceptable for "reflowable" books (books that automatically adjust to fit the screen on digital devices).

- **Print formats:** If you're publishing your book in print, 99% of the time you will need a ".pdf" file. This is the standard file type for any kind of print document, and most programs offer the option to export a file in this way.
- **Smashwords, Draft2Digital, Kobo, Apple, etc:** Most other publisher platforms and online services will solely request an ".epub" file for your book. If you only have a ".mobi" or a ".pdf" you can find online converters that will translate this file into an .epub for you.

Most programs should be able to convert your manuscript file into any and all of these formats for you to publish your book. All publishing platforms will also contain help guides and FAQs that should help navigate you through the process of publication if you do find yourself struggling.

Whatever method you use to format your book, one thing is fundamentally important: make your book *look* professional.

The reader experience happens primarily in the mind. When turning the first few pages, your reader will know to look for a copyright page or a contents page or a dedication page. They will know to look for "justified" text alignment and proper spacing. If your book fails to meet any of these standard expectations that have been prevalent in published books for years, you'll automatically be putting yourself at a disadvantage with your book. Your reader may not exactly know why, but they will understand that something is off.

For the best chances of success, make the interior of your book look like every other book that sits on your shelf.

9

IT IS TIME

OR "PUBLISHING YOUR BOOK"

> *Publishing a book is like stuffing a note into a bottle and hurling it into the sea. Some bottles drown, some come safe to land, where the notes are read and then possibly cherished, or else misinterpreted, or else understood all too well by those who hate the message. You never know who your readers might be.*
>
> — MARGARET ATWOOD

R afiki said it best. "It is time."
Man, I love *The Lion* King...

You've done the bulk of the grunt work. You've ground away to create the best damn book you can possibly make. You've broken your back and sweated until you were dry, all in the name of literature, and birthing your story to the world.

And it's here. It's ready to go.

But how do you get your book on the virtual bookshelves?

It's pretty easy, actually.

There are a number of major publishing platforms that make the process of getting your book onto the digital bookshelves as easy as uploading a Facebook album of your great aunt Sally's wedding. A couple of clicks of a button. A little bit of content input, and *BAM*! There it is, complete with Uncle Jensen vomiting on Great-Gran Mildred after too much champagne, little Jennifer stealing Oliver's table favors as he sobs his tears into his mother's dress, and the moment Sally's maid of honor got it off with her former father-in-law.

Ah, such a magical time.

Where were we?

Oh, right. Making your book live and available to purchase on your favorite online bookstore.

Where can you go?

Who are the major players in the online publishing realm?

The Big Guns
Or "The Platforms You Can't Ignore"

Kindle Direct Publishing (KDP): Amazon's pioneering KDP program was one of the first ever services to allow authors to self-publish directly onto the Amazon Kindle. After more than a decade of development, Amazon and its subsequent bookstore now hosts millions of books online and dominates the United States eBook market with roughly 75% of Americans choosing the Kindle as their e-reader of choice. It is one of the most popular book markets in the Western world, and a modern staple for any author looking to sell their book to the English-speaking masses.

> **PRO TIP:** After publishing your book on Amazon, make sure to "claim" your books and update your author profile on Amazon's Author Central service to look like a real pro on the sales page.

Kobo Writing Life (KWL): Rakuten's "Kobo" (an anagram of the word "book," I've *just* discovered) is one of the largest book retailers, boasting an audience of over 38 million users across 150+ countries. Users of the KWL platform can benefit from built-in promotional tools that allow authors to reach the right readers for their book at a very reasonable cost (sometimes for free).

Google Books: As with everything internet and life-related, Google has their grubby mitts in the eBook market too. A vastly growing market that conveniences readers with Android devices, Google Books may only hold a small corner of the world's market share of eBooks, but if we know anything about Google they'll be hell-bent on increasing that over time. Plus, it never hurts to have your books on more channels if you can.

Aggregate Services: If you're thinking, "I love the idea of having my books on all of these platforms, but doesn't that make it difficult to manage all of your books?" then have no fear.

There are a number of aggregate services out there which will take your book files and broadcast them to not only a whole host of online bookstores, but libraries, too. Here are just a few that are deservedly high in popularity among self-published authors.

- **Draft2Digital (D2D) and Smashwords:** If you're looking for an easy way to get your book onto the likes of Barnes & Noble, Apple Books, Scribd, Baker & Taylor, as well as a host of other platforms, then a service like Draft2Digital or Smashwords will make that happen for you.
- • **Ingram Spark:** Users of Ingram Spark can take advantage of their global distribution channels in publishing eBook, paperback, and hardback books. While users do have to pay an up-front fee per book published through the platform, Ingram currently provides one of the most effective ways to make beautiful hardbacks and to distribute paperbacks outside of the eBook ecosystems listed above.

Herald the Narrative, Dear Squire
Or "Publishing Your Audiobooks"

Although we haven't spoken all that much about the production of audiobooks, there are a number of ways to get these into the hands of narrators and to publish them on your favorite platforms.

Here's a brief rundown of some of the current options, although with audiobooks being one of the fastest-growing mediums at the moment, this is likely to expand as the years go by.

ACX: Yet another property owned by Amazon, ACX allows you to find narrators for your work and to publish the resulting audiobook on the Amazon Audible store. There are a number of options in terms of how payment and royalties work, with authors able to pay outright for their narrator's work or to arrange a royalty split. The latter will however bind you and the narrator into a seven-year exclusivity deal with ACX for that particular property.

Findaway Voices: Findaway are an audiobook aggregator in the same way that Draft2Digital, Smashwords, and Ingram are aggregators for their physical counterparts. With Findaway, you are able to source your own narrators and benefit from a number of royalty split and financial deals that don't bind you into exclusivity on any particular platform. You can also upload to Amazon through Findaway, as well as Apple, Google, Chirp, Hoopla, and Scribd, to name a few.

Kobo Writing Life: KWL allows you to publish your audiobooks directly to the Kobo platform. By going direct to their platform, you can take advantage of a number of exclusive promotional opportunities unavailable through third party distributors. With KWL you can also distribute your audiobook through Overdrive, Kobo's sister company, in order to get your book into the hands of libraries.

Speaking the Lingo
Or "Terminology for Your Upload"

Now that you've got the landscape of the options available at your fingertips, let's dive a little deeper into the nitty-gritty of the publishing jargon.

1. Book Details

- **Book title:** Nice and simple, what is your book going to be called?
- **Subtitle:** Not every book needs a subtitle, though if you have extra information you can always put it here. For example, on my anthologies I publish with other authors, I will often use this space to add, "A Horror Anthology," to make it clearer to the reader what they're buying (it doesn't hurt your "Search Engine Optimization" (SEO), too).
- **Series information:** Is your book part of a series? What's the name of that series? If you're not sure at this point, most platforms will let you leave this blank and come back later to edit when you add your second book.
- **Edition number:** It's likely this will be "1" or "First" for you at this point. If your book goes through any major reiterations (i.e. a whole new edit, updated chapters, new covers, etc.) you can then change this number to reflect this as your book goes through its life cycle.
- **Publisher name:** Who's publishing your book?

PRO TIP: Readers will subconsciously respond better to business names over personal names. My books are published by "Devil's Rock Publishing" which is my official business name, rather than "Daniel Willcocks."

- **Author:** What is your author name? If you're using a pen name, be sure to use this instead of your actual name.
- **Contributing authors:** Are you adding contributing authors to your book? Here you can credit everyone from your cover artist, to your editor, to someone who wrote an introduction for you. Note that any names you add here will be credited on your sales pages along with your name. Most authors tend to only link the names of the *major* contributors to the work and credit the rest of the team in the acknowledgements at the back.
- **Description:** Have you written your blurb yet? If so, this will go here. Your description of your book may start with a quote from a reader, or an enticing hook to draw the reader in.

PRO TIP: Tools such as Kindlepreneur's "Book Description Generator" can help to format your blurb in a way that looks professional on the sales pages and takes advantage of the platform's built-in HTML formatting. Simply drop in your blurb, format it on the site, then copy and paste the code to platforms such as KDP to make your description sing.

- **Categories:** These will dictate where your book "sits" on the Amazon bookshelf. In short, categories are aligned with your book's genre. Most stores let you select two options from a list of pre-designated categories. These can cover everything from "historical romance," to "space opera," to "non-fiction for authors." Ensure you choose the right categories for your book, so that the right readers can find you when they search.

- **Keywords:** I like to think of keywords as "flavor words." Your keywords are the complementary words that describe the type of book you've written. If you're searching for a brand-new car, you might use terms such as "fast," "economic," "yellow," to describe what you're looking for. Of course, these would be different to the categories of car which would be more representative of the make and model you're looking to buy (i.e. Mercedes, Ford, or Citroen). On most platforms you will be given seven spaces to put your keywords for your book. These will help your chosen platform find books when readers are getting more specific about what they choose to search for. I won't get too granular here, because this is a *whole* big kettle of fish, but if you want some great advice on keywords and how they work, there are a number of resources online and listed in the back of this book.

2. Book Content

ISBN: Your "International Standard Book Number" is the long string of digits that often sits above the barcode on the back of your books. It's an identifier that specifies the product type, country of origin, and publisher of your book, and you will require one if you are looking to publish physical books, such as paperbacks and hardbacks.

Some platforms, like KDP, offer free ISBNs, though if you're looking to make a career from your publishing, you should consider investing in your own set of ISBNs for your books. The rules for ISBNs and publication vary from country to country, with places like Canada offering free ISBNs to their citizens, so get familiar with how these work for you.

It's also worth noting that eBooks do not require an ISBN, so if you're only looking at publishing digitally, you can probably skip this step.

Digital Rights Management: Many platforms offer you the option of applying "DRM" to your book. This is simply an encryption process that is supposed to make it more difficult for people to edit, share, save, or forward your content outside of your chosen channels.

DRM is not a necessity when it comes to publishing your book, and it would benefit authors to do their own research to decide whether enabling DRM on your book is the right choice for you.

Publication date: Has this book been published previously? When would you like the book to go live? Some stores allow you to choose a date in which you can set your book available for pre-order, if you wish.

. . .

Print options:

- **Interior paper type:** What type of paper will be used inside your book? Mostly these choices filter down to cream or white paper. If you're not sure which is right for your book, look at your competitor books on your shelf and see what they use. Typically, most fiction books utilize cream paper, while many (though, not all) non-fiction books use white.
- **Trim size:** What size is your book going to be? You'll notice that the books sitting on your bookshelf come in an array of sizes. Trends change over time, though the most common standard book sizes are currently 5" × 8", 5.5" × 8.5", and 6" × 9".
- **Bleed settings:** A "bleed" is the spacing around the edge of the text on the page. It's the empty area that stops the text from covering every square inch of the page. This will vary depending on the type of book you're publishing. For the most part, written word books do not use a bleed, whereas books that are heavy in imagery, or sometimes poetry books tend to choose to apply the bleed around their work.
- **Paperback cover finish:** This is the type of finish used to apply to your book cover, often with the selection being between "matte" (flat, non-glossy cover), and "glossy" (smoother with a sheen to its finish). Similarly with your interior paper type, be deliberate about your choice of finish. Look at the books that you're trying to emulate and see what they use. The right finish on your book

cover can help your cover art sing and give your book that professional edge.

Upload cover: Does what it says on the tin. Upload your .jpeg, .png, or .pdf file for your book cover.

Upload manuscript: Drop in your .epub, .pdf, or .docX, depending on how you chose to format your book.

Previewer: This is a *crucial* step, and one that should never be missed. Although tedious, always be sure to launch the platform's built-in "Previewer" to see how your book will look on people's devices. I've caught many hidden errors this way, from missing pages, to wonky formatting, to glaring typos that missed the eagle eyes of editors. Go through, page-by-page, and ensure your book looks right and everything is as you planned. This is one of your last chances to ensure that your book is perfect before it ships out into the world.

PRO TIP: For an extra final check of your book, order a proof copy directly from your publisher of choice, and take a look through the physical print of your book before confirming that your book is final.

3. Book Pricing

Understanding your pricing strategy will be a key part of selling your book.

There are a number of approaches you could take with your pricing. eBooks tend to list at a lower price than your paperback. Paperbacks will be cheaper than your hardbacks. Audiobooks often cost the most.

If you're writing in a series, you could list your first book for free, and price the rest at $2.99. Or you could price the first at $1.99 and the rest at $3.99.

Research other books in your categories and understand their pricing structures. You can be experimental. However you decide to price your book, you can always change it. Optimize and keep moving. Test and see which works best for you.

NYBookEditors.com has a fantastic article titled, "How to Price Your Self-Published Book," which provides further information on pricing strategies for your book.

PRO TIP: Price yourself against other independent authors. Traditional publishing houses may be able to sell an eBook for $7.99, but you'll sure struggle.

You may find that your publishing platform has a few additional options when it comes to setting up your book, but these will cover you for the basics. If you hit a roadblock where you're unsure what a term means or what you're doing, most of the platforms provide fantastic help support and FAQ pages to help you get your book to publication.

Make Them Salivate
Or "Should I Set Up a Pre-Order?"

Depending on your launch strategy for your book, you will also be presented with the option of making your book available for pre-order before publication.

Pre-order strategies can be great when leveraged in the right way. By having your book available online before its release, you can promote the book more aggressively and build up those initial launch-day sales. It also makes it easier to schedule all of your promotion and plan things to go live at the right times because you have an active URL link you can send people to.

There are some pitfalls to pre-orders, however, depending on which platform you're using to publish. While platforms like Kobo and Apple store up those initial pre-order numbers and only count the sales on the day of your launch (increasing your overall ranking in the store due to sheer volume of sales), other stores, such as Amazon, count the sales from the day they come in. For example, if you have a slew of sales on your book thirty days before its release, those sales will be counted on the day they were made and won't contribute directly to your launch, thus potentially diminishing your total first day sales when those orders are confirmed and the books are sent to readers.

> **PRO TIP:** Check with your chosen platforms to find out how long each product takes to go live on eBook and print. You may have to time your launches to ensure that your print book goes live at the same time your eBook does.

As always, do your research and be deliberate about how you launch your book. I've listed some resources in the back of the book that may be helpful in informing your decision on pre-orders versus live publication.

You may find that your publishing platform of choice has a few additional options when it comes to publishing, but these will cover you for the basic information. If you hit a roadblock where you're unsure what a term means or what you're doing, most of the platforms provide fantastic help support and FAQ pages to help you get your book to publication.

You Can't Straddle the Two Camps
Or "Exclusive vs Wide"

One constantly ongoing debate in the indie author sphere is the discussion over "Should I be exclusive with my books, or should I be wide."

This is an age-old debate that has been around since the dawning of Amazon's "Kindle Unlimited" (KU) program—a subscription service that allows readers to pay a small monthly fee in return for access to an unlimited store of free online books. But what exactly does it mean?

When you publish your books, you essentially have two primary publication options that are dictated by the kinds of places you choose to publish, and the methods by which you wish to sell your books. In short, we can explain these two options as:

Exclusive

Your books are *exclusively* published through Amazon.

You can register your books for Amazon's "KDP Select" program which allows you to take advantage of a host of Amazon's premium features. Readers who are subscribed to Amazon's "Kindle Unlimited" program will be able to access your books for free, and you will benefit from a percentage of cashback for each page that is read through your book. Exclusive authors can take full advantage of Amazon promotions and algorithmic advantages to ensure that their books are being seen by Amazon's hungry, hungry reader-base.

If you choose this method, you will *not* be able to publish your books on other publishing platforms without breaking your Terms & Conditions with Amazon, which may end in a ban from the platform and removal of your books from the store.

However, one "term" with KDP Select only lasts for three months, so if you wanted to *try* this as a method of publication, you can do so for a three-month period. Once that three months has expired (provided you've actively selected the option to remove yourself from their auto subscribe), you'll be able to publish "wide" if you so choose.

Wide

Your books are *not* registered exclusively with Amazon, meaning you can publish on Amazon, Kobo, Google, Apple Books, and *anywhere* else you choose to publish them. You may not benefit from Amazon's KDP Select program, but you could reach more readers across more global territories with these different channels. You retain the rights to publish your book however you please.

There are many authors making a considerable living through Amazon exclusivity and riding the algorithms. However, there are also many authors who have found great success in publishing wide. There is no one way that is best for every author, but there are distinct pros and cons to each approach.

> **PRO TIP:** If you're worried about having to save multiple URLs to promote your book across the different platforms, you can use the books2read.com service to create a universal book link (UBL) so that you only need to send one link to your readers!

The pros of Exclusivity

- **Welcome to the KU Club:** The KU ecosystem is one of the most advanced reader subscription services in the world. KU readers form a huge percentage of Amazon's reader base, and exclusive authors have direct access to market their books at this ravenous pool.
- **All the promo!:** Baked within the KDP Select program are a bunch of free tools you can access every three months that allow you to promote your book to your readers. These include free book promotion days as well as "Countdown Deals."
- **Tapping the genre vein:** Genres with a voracious reader base benefit greatly from the KU program. Urban fantasy, space opera, and romance are just a few of the genres in which authors would do well to consider exclusivity.
- **75% of US readers are on Kindle:** With the United States being one of the largest English-speaking (and reading) countries on the planet, it

would behove any writer to consider aiming their books at this mammoth market.

- **Dip your toes:** Uploading your books to Amazon Kindle and allowing their algorithms to get you started in the KDP Select program *can* be an easier way for many authors to begin their self-publishing journey. Publishing exclusive can streamline your process and allow you to experiment with publishing on one of the major platforms before you move on to considering your next step.

The pros of Wide

- **No holds barred:** By choosing not to be exclusive with Amazon, you have unlimited options to publish your book. There are no barriers to stop you publishing your book on any of the other major global retailers, and you don't have to worry about breaking your T&Cs with Amazon just to get your books in the hands of readers. You're not bound by agreements that limit what goes where, and you reign supreme as the dominator of your intellectual property.
- **Promo, promo, promo!:** Certain advertising platforms would rather promote books that can be accessed by readers of all kinds than solely Amazon Kindle readers. Platforms such as BookBub.com actively favor books that are published wide, since their audience is readers from across *all* platforms. If you're publishing

directly to Kobo, you can also benefit from their free promotional opportunities, too.

- **We've gone global:** Amazon has a firm grasp on the US and UK markets, but there's a whole world of readers out there. Growing markets like Germany and India are seeing readers dive into the eBook economy, and platforms such as Kobo are your best way to start diversifying who reads your books. By not publishing exclusively, you could also sell the foreign rights to your books and have agents and international publishers market your books for you in the countries where you otherwise would not be able to confidently publish.

- **Ten eggs, ten baskets:** This is the key one for many authors. By publishing on multiple platforms, you form a failsafe for if any of your other platforms change their rules or stop paying you. At the click of their fingers, Amazon *could* change their payment structure, meaning that, should you have been earning 70% of your $30,000 income, you could now be earning 20% and making just $6,000 instead of your $21,000. By putting yourself on multiple platforms, and diversifying your income, you allow yourself to stay in the game longer, and worry less about changes you cannot control.

- **The tortoise beat the hare:** The wide method can sometimes be a slow burn, but those who stick at it, and do well, see steady, continual growth in sales and income. By building a reputation as an author who can be accessed on any device, store, or platform, you can make a good, stable living this way.

The cons of Exclusivity

- **75% of _US_ readers are on Kindle:** The world isn't just made up of the United States. There's a whole sea of readers all waiting to see your books in their hands. If you want a truly global readership, this may not be the path for you.
- **Ten eggs, one basket:** If all your income comes from Amazon, what happens when they change the rules?
- **The small print:** While Amazon has many benefits, there have been many questions around the transparency of Amazon's Terms & Conditions. Some authors have had their accounts closed without so much as a word of warning, and though this is rare, this is a terrible position for authors to find themselves in.

The cons of Wide

- **Juggling dashboards:** By putting yourself on more platforms, you have more dashboards to keep an eye on. Updating your prices on your books no longer becomes a visit to a single website, it becomes a half hour process of going through all the platforms and ensuring that they are all saying the same things.
- **On the outside looking in:** You won't be able to benefit from the KU reader pool. Nuff said.

No matter whether you decide to go exclusive or wide with your books, Amazon will be a definitive player in your publication journey. The choice then becomes whether you choose for them to be the *dominate* player, or a *complementary* player in your publishing empire.

> **PRO TIP:** If you'd like to find out more about publishing publishing Wide, a fantastic resource is Mark Leslie Lefebvre's *Wide for the Win*.

10

A SQUARE PEG FOR A SQUARE HOLE

OR "MARKETING FOR AUTHORS"

"Marketing" your book. *Shudder.*
Does it fill you with fear?
Does it fill you with excitement?

Marketing your book can be difficult for some, and remarkably easy for others. You'll be sick of me saying this by now but, as with many of the stages of self-publication, the *right* way to market your book doesn't exist. It's highly individualized, and the good news is that there are a thousand ways to get your books into the hands of readers.

All you need to do is find the one that works for you.

Our Eyes Met Across the Crowded Room
Or "The Ideal Reader: Revisited"

Before we dive into the nitty gritty of tactics and methods to sell your book, I wanted to touch on a note that I've mentioned a few times throughout the book, but which is *fundamental* if you want to make a long-term, sustainable living with your writing.

You *must* target the *right* readers.

You've worked hard this far to ensure that your cover and your story are aimed at readers of the right genre. You've set your categories and keywords appropriately to make sure that you're bringing in the readers who will love *you* and all that *you* do.

Now's not the time to start splatter-gunning your book into the void.

Marketing can be messy, unpredictable, and fun. Want to know the best way to ensure you're not wasting your time with all of your marketing efforts?

Reach the *right* readers.

It's much more effective to secure 50 readers onto your mailing list who will buy everything you do, than to round up 1,500 readers who only joined your mailing list to win a free Kindle.

Be deliberate.

Be targeted.

Marketing doesn't have to be difficult, and if you do it well you can generate a solid reader base of people who love the work *you* do. I've made a career from slowly building a solid reader base of fans who like the content I put out. I've never resorted to cheap tactics to flood my list with subscribers. Is it effective to have a list of 10,000 readers when only 1% of them are actually buying your books?

Probably not.

Build a solid reader base, and you will make it in this industry. Kevin Kelly has a fantastic essay about this strategy titled, "1,000 True Fans." Seth Godin talks constantly about finding your "Minimum viable audience." Both discussions advocate the benefits of building a small, rabid fanbase over a colossal, unwieldy, half-interested fan club.

Think about it. Would you rather have 20 people at your

birthday party who care about you and actually seem bothered to ask you questions, or would you rather a stadium of strangers who couldn't give a damn whether you were there?

Find the *right* readers.

Treat them well.

Give them what they want—that is to say: *you*.

I Can't Time Travel, Karen!
Or "When Should I Begin Marketing?"

The choice is yours.

The journey of marketing your book can begin at any time of your journey. I don't just mean throwing out pretty images on social media, I mean laying the foundations of an author platform and getting the tools in place so that you're ready to catch those readers when you do eventually launch your book.

It can also begin months *after* releasing your book (though I wouldn't necessarily recommend this). If you've been paralyzed with fear of people critiquing your book, or your mother seeing that slightly raunchy sex scene you put toward the end of chapter fourteen, you may be hesitant to actually shout about your book at all—y'know, until you realize you actually *wanted* people to read the book, which was the whole point of all of this in the first place.

All of this is to say that marketing your book is an agile process. Authors will make their own way with promotion and getting to grips with the tools you are comfortable with. There's a whole raft of strategies and methods out there, and they deserve a full book's worth of content to explore. For now, let's consider some basic questions you may be asking.

Does it make a difference if you begin marketing sooner rather than later?

Yes. Absolutely.

If you don't market your book until months after it's released, will it affect sales?

Yes. In the beginning at least, you'll have a much slower climb to seeing substantial return on your income.

Is it impossible to market an old book that hasn't been touched in years?

No.

No matter what stage of the journey you're at, you can find a way to get your books into the hands of readers and start generating income. The methods and the mileage may vary, but it *is* possible. It all depends how hard you're willing to work.

It's All About the Journey
Or "Marketing Before You've Written Your Book"

Marketing your book can start before you even set your fingers to the keyboard.

Some authors thrive off bringing people along on their *journey* of writing their masterpiece. Social media platforms are filled with writers sharing pictures of their writing spaces, the routines they're building to get the words in, their author influences, the development of their characters, plot, mood boards, etc. Blogs are packed with in-depth notes surrounding the types of story structure that are available to authors, and the "ideal morning routine," to get your words on the page.

The *journey* is special.

The *journey* is fascinating.

Do you know how many people *want* to write a book? Do you know how many people start their book but never finish?

Well, you should. I told you earlier. Nice to know you've been paying attention.

(If you *did* know the answer, I'm sorry. Please forgive me. I make an incredible Terry's Chocolate Orange Cheesecake. It's already in the mail and on its way to you.)

In Austin Kleon's bestselling book, *Show Your Work*, he talks in great depth about how you can build a following just through the process of creation.

> *Audiences not only want to stumble across great work, but they too, long to be creative and part of the creative process.*

Think about it: wouldn't you have loved to see how the Mona Lisa was painted? What kind of paints did da Vinci use? Did he sketch an outline first? How long did it take? What if you could have been a *part* of the process, cheering them on and being there as some of the world's most famous paintings unfolded before your eyes?

What about *The Handmaid's Tale*, or *The Shining*, or [insert your favorite book of choice here]? Doesn't it feel a little special to gain a behind-the-scenes glance and see it all come together?

Document what you do. If you're in the process of learning: share that. Bestselling author of *The Savior's Champion*, Jenna Moreci, started her YouTube channel months *before* she'd released her debut novel. She documented her learning journey, she shared tips along the way, and now she has a number of chart-smashing books she can sell to her audience of 250,000 viewers. Wherever you are in your journey, there are thousands of people out there either fascinated by what you're doing, or willing to learn from you—mistakes, warts, and all.

It may be a slow burn. You may find that you have ten followers after three months of sharing content—but that's ten more than you originally had.

That, my friend, is called growth.

"But Dan, *how* do I document *my* process?"

We, as humans, connect with the things that regularly appear in our lives. I know that my own social media feeds are full of hustlers getting the work done. The ones that I follow the closest are the ones who share their content regularly, and who share *generously*.

A daily snippet of your journey is more powerful than a weekly one. A weekly share is more powerful than monthly —but choose what works best for you when it comes to creating your schedule and sharing your content. *You* set your expectations, and your readers will follow.

I try to share a little something every day. My chosen platform at the minute is Instagram, and every day I share a little something that gives a behind-the-scenes of what I'm up to. By sharing snippets and previews of upcoming work, I can keep readers curious and interested. If authors are following me, they can see my raw, unfiltered process and feel safe knowing that the process is messy and irregular and tough.

Share the "real," people!

Houston, We Have Lift-off
Or "Launching Your Book"

The day you launch your book can trigger a cocktail of emotions. You may find yourself ecstatic, terrified, excited, or anxious at the prospect that you're now able to put your book into the hands of readers.

But how do you build up to your promotion? How do you get readers excited about the story you're going to present them with, without sounding like a disingenuous, greasy salesperson standing at your door with a battered brochure and a suitcase full of kitchen knives?

There are a few rules and tricks of the trade that can help.

I. **Don't Be Sleazy:** There's nothing worse than authors relentlessly shouting, "Buy my book," into the void. You will lose followers, and you will piss people off. People *want* to buy your book, but they don't want to do it because you told them. They want to do it because *they're* interested.

I used to hate cleaning my room as a kid. No matter how many times my mother shouted at me to do so, I never gleaned any enjoyment from it. Yet, years on (and after the healing of many mental scars) I actually quite enjoy the process of cleaning. I like having a tidy room and a clean house. I understand why my mother so diligently beat that horse and emphasized making my areas of the house appear fresh and clean.

Perhaps I would have come to the realization sooner if she hadn't have shouted so much. If I had been allowed to approach the process of cleaning in my own way, and understood the value of what she was teaching, I would have happily cleaned my room.

Do you see the analogy I'm trying to draw, here?

Let the readers come to you. Share the things that are

tangible that *you* are excited about that *they could* get excited about, too. Give them their own reasons to follow you, without constantly yelling at a brick wall and expecting it to move.

2. Build the Hype: Hype up your excitement about your book launch. Talk about the readers who have already seen snippets and are loving it (yeah, FOMO works for marketing). If you're sharing a behind-the-scenes image, keep it positive and exciting. Things like, "Can't wait for you all to read this," and "I'm incredibly happy with how this is turning out," provides much more buzz than, "I hope everything goes okay," or "I'm questioning the plot and the cover design."

3. Cover Reveals: Revealing the cover image of your book can be one of the most powerful tools you have at your disposal. Artwork gets people excited and seeing a shiny new book cover can really get the adrenaline pumping for readers.

A couple of quick tips for cover reveals:

- **Time them well:** If you reveal your book cover eight months ahead of the book's release, the excitement will have died before your book is available to the public. All that momentum you build settles on the ground with nowhere for your readers to purchase their book or sort their pre-order. Share the cover in the final weeks leading up to your publication date for maximum effect.

- **Teasing the cover:** There are templates available online to show a teaser of the cover's art. Don't show the full image, just wet the lips of those waiting to read your book.
- **Pre-orders:** If you're looking at making your book available for pre-order, you can time this with your cover reveal for maximum effect. If your reader is buzzing with excitement for your book, give them a button they can click to actually order the damn thing.

4. Sharing Excerpts: If you've got particular paragraphs, sentences, or phrases that you're proud of that you think will entertain readers, then share them! Be sure you don't give the plot away, but leverage the content to introduce your characters, your tone, and to show off your literary prowess.

5. Media Appearances: There are a number of podcasts, radio shows, magazines, and other media outlets that are always excited to talk to working authors. You don't need to have yet published to contact these shows, but you will need to show that you are serious about the craft and that you *will* release an end product. Appearing across various mediums will allow you to build your reputation as a professional author, and start to generate a following. Sometimes it's as simple as finding the show's website and getting in contact. Be prepared for no's, but amidst those no's you will find a number of yes's.

PRO TIP: Be deliberate about the media opportunities you apply for. Is your audience actually there? What will *you* get from this opportunity?

Take the time to write a plan for your marketing. Know what you're trying to achieve (I refer you to Chapter 1) and work your strategy toward that goal. The more attention you pay before you start to promote, the more effective your marketing will be, and the greater the chance you will have to reach the right readers and increase your sales.

A Woollen Hammer for a Glass Nail
Or "Fundamental Tools of Author Marketing"

Your Author Website

We are now at a point in time where it's ridiculously easy to put together a simple, professional website to host your author profile. In the beginning, all you need is a simple one-page site that tells the world who you are, what you do, and what you're working on. Your website will be an always-in-progress asset to you, creating a central portal where you can promote your work and point readers toward so they can find out more about you. If you time your website build well, you can also include this into your marketing strategy to promote your work and get readers into your funnel.

PRO TIP: Pay attention to the options provided by your web provider to improve your "SEO." Search Engine Optimization makes it easier for search engines such as Google and Safari to find your website and your links. Although you may not choose to become an expert in SEO, it will benefit you to pay attention to the small things you can do that will make it easier for readers to find you.

Your Author Mailing List

Ask any author and they will tell you the most powerful tool you have at your disposal is your author mailing list.

It's great having a platform on social media, but we've already seen that social platforms come and go with the trends. We've seen the likes of Vine disappear, and the beast that was Snapchat fade into near-nothingness. Algorithms behind the scenes change over time, and soon what was once working for you on TikTok won't be effective in your marketing anymore.

That's where mailing lists come in.

Your mailing list is *your* mailing list. Email and its functionality hasn't changed all that much since the 80s, and it likely won't in the coming decade.

(Crosses fingers and waits for Dan-from-the-future to tell me I'm wrong... No? All good? Good.)

Having your readers' email addresses gives you a direct line of contact from author to reader. There's no middle person, there are no blocks or barriers. If you can build a strong mailing list of readers, you will be able to build a sustainable author career—1,000 eager fans waiting to buy your next book the moment you send out an email is pure gold. You *need* a mailing list in this industry, at this time in the world's history.

So, get one.

I'm not going to create a huge list of email providers, because there are a tonne, and they all have their pros and cons. Personally, I use MailerLite because it does all that I need it to do. I've used MailChimp in the past, I've heard great things about AWeber, and there are plenty more out there I could mention. You'll need to do your research to find out what works best for you.

Reader Magnets

Your reader magnet is a tool that links directly with your mailing list.

In layman's terms, a reader magnet is a short story or novella that you offer your readers for free in exchange for their email address. It's a "hook" that gets readers onto your list so you can start building a relationship with them.

A reader magnet can be anything from a single page PDF, to a short story, to a novella, to a full novel. *You* decide what you're happy to give away for free. If you plan your reader magnet carefully, you can coincide this to launch with your website ahead of your book's release and start bringing fans onto your list months ahead of your book's release.

My advice: make sure the reader magnet links strongly with the book you're writing. I'm not going to give away a six-page pamphlet on the best seeds to plant in the Louisiana Spring to get people on a list where I'll be sending them the link to download my hard crime thriller. What I will do is write a short story about a character that appears within my main novel, giving readers a side story that relates heavily to the plot of my book.

Want to find out where Jonah got his were-powers? Want to see what happened when the apocalypse first hit our protagonist's love interest? Love the comic relief that Sabrina brings to the story? Well then, why not find out where she discovered her comedy bone in this rapid, page-turning novella!

Whatever the scenario, it will play in your favor to tie the reader magnet in with your book. This applies for both fiction and non-fiction books.

Choose wisely.

Choose well.

A Word on Social Media

Notice that I didn't put down social media as a fundamental tool of marketing.

While social media certainly *can* play its part in selling books, I've known a fair number of authors who simply don't use this in their marketing strategy. If social media is not your thing, then you are not wholly restricted by this. There are alternate methods out there. Will they be as powerful and as effective as social media promotion? That's up to you. How hard are you willing to work?

If social media *is* your thang, then hooray, honey. You've got this in the bag.

Forming Your Band of Superfans
Or "Beta Readers, Street Teams, and ARC Readers"

Now *this* is where it gets fun.

As a self-published author, you don't have the backing of large conglomerates to promote your work and to help you build a loyal reader base. That pleasure comes down to you.

Many authors form Street Teams, Advanced Reader Copy (ARC) groups, and Beta Reader teams for their books. Each serves a slightly different purpose, but the core principle is this: these are a small, exclusive group of readers who enjoy your work and are willing to give honest feedback to help you as an author.

- **Beta readers:** These are readers who read early drafts of your work to provide reader feedback ahead of any major edits. We've covered these already, but beta readers can be useful when working through tough plot points or if you're insecure about particular characters. Having real readers give you their opinion at the right time is priceless. Just be sure that the opinion reaches a consensus and that you aren't just scratching one reader's specific itch. Beta readers, when sourced well, can also feed into your ARC team and Street teams, too.
- **Street teams:** Readers within your street team are advocates for you and all you do. They will share your posts, they will promote your books on their channels, they will provide social proof to other readers that you're worth investing their time in. They're akin to a rabid fan group who are there to help you do well.
- **ARC readers:** ARC readers who are willing to read your book in exchange for an *honest* review of your work on launch day. Reviews are the lifeblood of authors, providing social evidence that your book is worth picking up. Having a team of readers who can provide 10+ ratings for you on the stores on the day of your launch can *significantly* help your launch day sales, as well as tickle the algorithms enough for certain

platforms to rank you higher and show your
work to more readers.

The great thing about these kinds of reader teams is that many readers will happily help out for free. They're receiving free (digital) copies of your books, and they're influencing the launch of something special.

That's a pretty cool thing to be a part of.

But How Do you Source Readers to Help You?

Well, the answer is laid out above. Build your following, whether that's on Facebook, or YouTube, or through your mailing list, and then just ask.

It's that simple.

Find the readers who are excited to invest in your work. You'll be surprised how many will jump at the chance to be a part of your process and get some free stuff. Sure, you may find that a few of those readers are duds who don't help you at all (believe me, I've been there), but you can cut them from your groups easily enough. It's all about trial and error, and the further through the process you get, the stronger your team will become.

Be sure to treat your readers fairly. Remember that they're helping you out—for free. Remember that they are people, too, with busy lives and drama and daydreams. Don't badger them and expect them to move Heaven and Earth for you. Be patient. Be kind. Make it a good experience to work with you and provide praise and feedback to *them* if you find their contributions helpful.

Your reader teams can become an incredibly strong community of friends, with you sitting at the center of it all. Their input will be reflected by how you treat them, so don't take them for granted. They're doing something amazing for you, and you're giving them something amazing in return.

> **PRO TIP:** I always ensure that I personally thank every one of my ARC readers at the beginning of my books by name. I want them to know I care about them and I'm thankful for their input.

And you don't even *need* to have all of these teams. I currently have a strong ARC team to help me out when I launch books, and that's it. I'll be playing around with a Street team soon to boost the books after they launch, but it's down to the author to decide what works best for them. It can take time and energy to cultivate a whole cohort of avid fans.

It can also be vastly rewarding, too.

A Necessary Evil
Or "Paid Advertising"

Oh, yes.

We're there.

The monster in the pit.

The cash hungry creature at the bottom of the chasm.

Ravenous.

Insatiable.

Necessary?

Perhaps.

As effective as all of the above is with marketing and promoting your book, I'd be lying if I said you wouldn't have to put *some* skin in the game if your goal for writing your book is to make stacks of that circular, metal stuff that clinks in wallets and weighs down the dead one's eyes.

As self-publishing markets have matured, more and more people have flooded to the platforms to sell their books. Publishing is business—*big* business—and it's always worth remembering that it is within the best interest of these businesses to be making money.

CPC Advertising

Cost-per-click (CPC) advertising is the investment of a portion of your budget into platforms such as Facebook Business, Amazon Marketing Services (AMS), or BookBub in order for the business to prioritize your books in their listings. These platforms will take your ad spend and use it to promote your book to readers. For every successful click of a reader on your product, you will be charged accordingly.

If you type in any author's name on Amazon, you will find a number of their books appear in the search. You will also, inevitably, find a number of sponsored books from other authors.

That's where your CPC ads position you.

CPC advertising is a whole subject to learn in itself, and there are dozens of courses and professionals out there who can teach you far better than I ever will. Below are a number of places you can start if you're looking at getting involved with paid marketing platforms:

- Mark Dawson's "Advertising for Authors" course
- David Gaughran's *BookBub Ads Expert*
- Chris Fox's *Ads for Authors Who Hate Math*
- Brian D. Meeks' *Mastering Amazon Ads*

- Mal Cooper and Jill Cooper's *Help! My Facebook Ads Suck: Second Edition*
- Bryan Cohen's "5-Day Amazon Ad Profit Challenge"

No matter what platform you choose to master first, know that those who are making the big bucks are at least dabbling in CPC advertising platforms.

One-Shot Promotions

If CPC sounds like too much work for you, or you're intimidated to start your work there, there are other platforms that will take a single one-off payment in order to promote your work.

Newsletter promotional sites such as E-reader News Today (ENT), Book Barbarian, and Robin Reads are all examples of websites where, for a one-time fee, you can get your book into the hands of thousands of readers.

For as low a cost as $30, you can send these sites your book information and schedule a date for them to promote your book to their list of avid readers. For most of these sites, they do expect you to discount your book, or set it up for a free promotion, but it's a great way to get your book into the hands of new and excited readers.

Mailing lists can successfully be built this way, as long as you have your mailing list link at the end of your book and you're leveraging your reader magnet to keep those readers interested in your work. It can also do wonders in creating a "spike" in your sales which will boost your book ranking.

PRO TIP: Create a sustainable spike by setting up a number of promotions over a few days in close succession. Let your book ride the algorithmic wave for a week to see longer-lasting results on your sales and ranking.

There are many more methods and strategies that can guide your marketing efforts, but to list them all would create a body of work that rivaled James Joyce's *Ulysses*.

Marketing is agile, it's fluid, it's big. Start with one thing and do that thing well before you expand. You *don't need* to be on every social media platform if you don't understand them all.

Experiment.

Find what works for you.

Nail that thing and then move on to the next.

The list of possible marketing avenues is limitless, and you may find your own brand-new niche that has never been discovered and slays all expectations.

For now, these are the fundamentals of what you will need to know to market your book. Anything beyond this is considered extra credit, and you won't need to see me after class.

11

WHAT COMES NEXT?

W rite the next book.

12

NO, REALLY. WHAT COMES NEXT?

S eriously.
  Write the next book.

13

ANSWER THE QUESTION, DAN!

F ine.
    Calm down.
Allow me to elaborate.

 Nothing sells the last book like the next book.

Congratulations on completing your first full cycle of self-publishing. You'll likely be exhausted. You may be elated. That sense of achievement that comes from creating art and releasing it *on your own* is monolithic and should not be underestimated.

You've done an amazing thing.

Publishing houses employ entire teams for this kind of stuff. They have marketers and directors and proofreaders and printers and financial advisors and janitors and delivery teams and assistants and reception staff, and you've done all of that yourself?

Dude...

This is one of the reasons I love self-publishing. It's

taking everything into your own hands and creating the impossible. You're a one-person band creating a symphony. You're a lone engineer creating a working car from scratch.

You did it.

You did it!

But now what happens?

What happens at the end of *every* cycle?

We begin again.

You may have found this process so tiring that it seems impossible to do it again, and that's okay. Self-publishing *isn't* for everyone.

You may find that you wish to continue writing but you'd rather pursue the traditional route next time—agents, and all. You may wish to give up writing altogether. You tried it, and it didn't work for you.

That's okay, too.

But, for those rare few among us who find ourselves energized at handcuffing ourselves to the wheel of torture and beginning the process again, that process starts *now*.

The cycle is endless, and it is unchanging. No matter how many books you write, no matter the types of books you publish, in order to create the best product that *you* are capable of writing, you must abide by this cycle.

Skip a step and suffer the consequences.

Y'know, suffer alone...

I'm not going to be holding a branding iron to your ass cheeks. That's not my style, plus I'm already late for my sister's birthday party.

PRO TIP: The more books you have stacked in your "backlist," the more chances readers have to find you. Self-publishing is a game of exponential growth. If a reader finds you when you have one book, you may make $2 from that sale. If your reader finds you when you have twenty books to your name, and they buy every one, that's $40—that's a 1,900% increase in profit from one reader.

That's the key to longevity and sustainability in this career, my friend. Great quality books, and many of them.

Onward, Young Adventurer
Or "A Final Word Before You Go"

So, there it is. We've covered the self-publishing journey from start to finish. I've given you a full overview of the fundamentals of what it takes to get your books from that impressive mind of yours to the digital and physical bookshelves.

No matter what your publishing goal, you should be able to start your adventure now with less anxiety and more knowledge of the stepping stones that you will need to cross. We've shone a light on the ogres, and we've explored the pit stops you'll make along the way. The road will be long, and it may be difficult, but it will be worth it in the end.

There's nothing like holding a book that you've written in your hands. To smell the paper, to see the words written in ink (or e-ink) before you, and to know that other people are reading your creation across the world.

But the only way to make that happen is to get started.

So, go ahead.

It's time.

You're ready.

Go get 'em, kid. Get to writing, and start your self-publishing journey today.

THANKS (AND BONUS CONTENT)

Thank you for taking the time to read *The Self-Publishing Blueprint*. If you want some extra goodies, then you're in the right place.

Free Self-Publishing Checklist

Download your FREE checklist to track your publishing journey.

https://danielwillcocks.com/blueprint

Write with Dan!

Did you know I run an online writing community with authors and creatives? Join me for live writing sprints, guest Q&As, and monthly socials.

https://danielwillcocks.com/community

Need help with that story?

Sometimes all the courses and conferences aren't enough to help *you* with *your* specific situation. If you're looking for an extra hand, why not check out my book coaching services, to see if I can guide you through the troubled waters of publishing in a 1-on-1 environment?

https://danielwillcocks.com/help

One last ask...

If you've enjoyed this book, please consider leaving a review. Reviews are the lifeblood of independent authors, and we can't thank you enough for showing other readers what you thought of the book. Even just a star rating can go a looooong way.

ACKNOWLEDGMENTS

As I wrote within the pages you've (presumably) already read, this book wouldn't have been born without a crucial cocktail of writers who came into my life over the last six months and have continued to transform my process and how I approach the world of storytelling.

A huge thank you to my coaching clients, who not only take the plunge in trusting me with the incredible worlds they're creating, but who also challenge my knowledge and help me see through the eyes of a 'young' writer again. This book was born from the curiosity, challenges, and complications which arise from the publishing process, and is my answer to the repeat questions which I face on a (nearly) weekly basis.

Thank you to the amazing writers in my Willcocks Writers' group, who turn up each and every week and put in the hard work to make the stories that this world needs to read. Not only do I hold you all to account, but you certainly shine that mirror my way and keep me on the path to continual betterment. Let this book be a personalized guide for each of your journeys as you carry forth down one of the hardest roads we can face.

Thank you (again) to the rebel queen herself, Sacha Black, for inspiring my non-fiction and continuing to challenge the truths I once believed about myself.

Thank you to Katlyn Duncan and Crys Cain whose constant support throughout this writing malarkey is never taken for granted, and who both educate me to be a better Queen.

And, at last, thank you to the reader, for without your eyes on this page, I may as well be living in invisibility. If you've taken the plunge to self-publish your book, know that you're brave, pioneering, bold, and true, and if you've got the courage to get your books out into the hands of strangers, then you've got the strength to do anything, my friend.

Until next we meet.
Daniel Willcocks
26 April 2021

ABOUT THE AUTHOR

Daniel Willcocks is an international bestselling author and award-nominated podcaster of dark fiction. He is one fifth of digital story studio, Hawk & Cleaver; co-founder of iTunes-busting fiction podcast, 'The Other Stories';' CEO of horror imprint, Devil's Rock Publishing; and the co-host of the 'Next Level Authors' podcast

Dan is furiously passionate about all things story. He has written 40+ books in four years for himself and on behalf of ghostwriting clients. Dan also provides book coaching services designed to help authors take the stories that they are dying to tell, and getting them out onto the page.

Visit www.danielwillcocks.com to find out more.

facebook.com/willcocksauthor

twitter.com/willcocksauthor

instagram.com/willcocksauthor

RESOURCES

MARKET RESEARCH

- **K-lytics** https://k-lytics.com/
- **Publisher Rocket** https://publisherrocket.com/

CRAFT

- **Anatomy of Prose** by Sacha Black
- **Consider This** by Chuck Palahnuik
- **How to Write Non-fiction** by Joanna Penn
- **On Writing** by Stephen King
- **Save the Cat** by Blake Snyder
- **Take Off your Pants** by Libby Hawker
- **Three Story Method** by J Thorn and Zach Bohannon

FORMATTING

- **Amazon's "Kindle Create"**
- https://www.amazon.com/Kindle-Create/b?ie=UTF8&node=18292298011
- **PublishDrive's "Ebook Converter"** https://converter.publishdrive.com/

- **Reedsy's "Write A Book"** https://reedsy.com/write-a-book

PUBLISHING

- **ACX** https://acx.com
- **Books2Read** https://books2read.com/
- **Draft 2 Digital** https://draft2digital.com
- **Findaway Voices** https://findawayvoices.com
- **Google Play** https://play.google.com/books/publish
- **Ingram Spark** https://ingramspark.com
- **Kindle Direct Publishing** https://kdp.amazon.com
- **Kobo Writing Life** https://kobo.com/us/en/p/writinglife
- **Smashwords** https://smashwords.com
- **Wide for the Win** by Mark Leslie Lefebvre

MARKETING

Courses and Further reading

- **1,000 True Fans** by Kevin Kelly
- https://kk.org/thetechnium/1000-true-fans/
- **Ads for Authors Who Hate Math** by Chris Fox
- **BookBub Ads Expert** by David Gaughran
- **Bryan Cohen's 5-Day Amazon Ad Profit Challenge**
- https://www.facebook.com/groups/2230194167089012/

- **Help! My Facebook Ads Suck: Second Edition** by Mal Cooper and Jill Cooper
- **Mark Dawson's Ads for Authors**
- https://courses.selfpubform.com/referral/adsforauthors/OKgoJPhYYk8y3EHf
- **Mastering Amazon Ads** by Brian D. Meeks

Mailing List Providers

- **AWeber** https://www.aweber.com/
- **Mailchimp** https://mailchimp.com/
- **Mailerlite** https://www.mailerlite.com/

Keywords and Categories

- **The Creative Penn "Book Categories & Keywords** https://www.thecreativepenn.com/book-categories-keywords/

CPC Advertising

- **Amazon Marketing Services** https://advertising.amazon.com/
- **BookBub** https://www.bookbub.com/ebook-deals/recommended
- **FB Business** https://business.facebook.com/

Newsletter Resources

- **How To Promote A Book (Using Sites & Services That Work)** https://scribemedia.com/book-promotion-sites/

- **Book Funnel** https://bookfunnel.com/
- **Prolific Works** https://www.prolificworks.com/
- **Story Origin** https://storyoriginapp.com/

OTHER TITLES BY DANIEL WILLCOCKS

Non-fiction for Authors

Collaboration for Authors

The Self-publishing Blueprint

Fiction

They Rot (The Rot: Book 1)

They Remain (The Rot: Book 2)

When Winter Comes

Twisted: A Collection of Dark Tales

The Mark of the Damned

Sins of Smoke

Anthologies

The Other Side

The Omens Call

Keep up-to-date at

www.danielwillcocks.com